Microwave
Miracles

FROM

Microwave Miracles

FROM

Sears

A Rutledge Book
The Benjamin Company, Inc.
New York, New York

by Hyla O'Connor

ISBN: 0-87502-042-9
Library of Congress Catalog Card Number: 74-81126
Prepared and produced by The Ridge Press, Inc.—Rutledge Books Division
Published by The Benjamin Company, Inc.
485 Madison Avenue
New York, New York 10022
Printed in Japan
13th Printing 1979

All photographs by Walter Storck Studios, Inc.
Illustrations by Tom Huffman

Microwave Miracles

FROM

Sears

USER INSTRUCTIONS

**PRECAUTIONS TO AVOID POSSIBLE EXPOSURE TO
EXCESSIVE MICROWAVE ENERGY**

(a) DO NOT ATTEMPT to operate this oven with the door open since
open-door operation can result in harmful exposure to microwave
energy. It is important not to defeat or tamper with the safety
interlocks.

(b) DO NOT PLACE any object between the oven front face and the
door or allow soil or cleaner residue to accumulate on sealing
surfaces.

(c) DO NOT OPERATE the oven if it is damaged. It is particularly
important that the oven door closes properly and that there is no
damage to the:
(1) DOOR (bent)
(2) HINGES AND LATCHES (broken or loosened)
(3) DOOR SEALS AND SEALING SURFACES.

(d) THE OVEN SHOULD NOT BE ADJUSTED OR REPAIRED BY
ANYONE EXCEPT PROPERLY QUALIFIED SERVICE
PERSONNEL.

Contents

Enjoy Your Sears Automatic Defrost Features

The Sears Automatic Defroster

Microwave Defrosting

Your Automatic Defroster provides unparalleled ease and convenience for defrosting frozen foods. Microwave energy heats the outer section of the food, and this heat is conducted toward the center. Without automatic defrosting, there is danger of overheating the outside of the food before the center is defrosted. Automatic defrosting provides a slower, more gentle heating that allows heat to be conducted toward the center of the food.

Defrost Cooking

In addition to defrosting, the Automatic Defroster was designed to provide new convenience and flexibility in microwave cooking. Because of its controlled heating, Defroster is ideal for use in cooking certain types of foods — especially those that require more time to bring out their tenderness and flavor. The following recipes have been developed since the printing of the cookbook.

Take a little time to become familiar with the Automatic Defroster and you'll be amazed at what it can do to increase your enjoyment of foods cooked in your microwave oven.

More than a Defroster

The controlled heating makes defrosting as easy as pushing a button. But also you can:
HEAT LEFTOVERS — The controlled heat makes it easy to warm the center of any leftover without overcooking its edges. This guide includes an entire page of ideas to simplify the heating of refrigerated and frozen prepared foods.
SIMMER FOODS — When a food mixture is just about to boil, Defrost can be turned on and the mixture will slowly simmer.
COOK FOODS MORE EVENLY — The gentle heating improves some baked goods by evenly warming the batter first, so that it will cook quickly when the regular "cook cycle" is used. With large cuts of meat, automatic defrosting allows cooking heat to reach the center without overcooking the edges. With custard mixtures, the slower cooking sets the center and prevents boiling of the edges or separating of the custard.

Meat Defrosting Guide

Use this guide for easy defrosting of meat, poultry, fish and seafood. For other meat items, compare with a meat of similar size and shape. Most meats will still be a little icy in the center after defrosting. For the juiciest cooked meats it is best to have a little ice in the center when beginning to cook.

For additional information refer to the reheating guide on the next page of this booklet. Foods that require less than one minute of defrosting are best defrosted manually rather than with the Automatic Defrost.

Since there are several variables that can affect defrost time, you may find it necessary to adjust slightly the times given in this chart.

Meat Defrosting Guide

Meat Item	Size	Defrost Times	Special Helps
Meat			
Ground Beef	1 lb.	About 7 min.	As the outside defrosts, break off the defrosted part and return the frozen part to the oven.
	1½ lbs.	About 10 min.	
	2 lbs.	About 14 min.	
Blade Roast, 2 inches thick	5 lbs.	17 min.; rest 5 min.; about 7 min.	
Rolled Rib Roast	3½ lbs.	16 min.; rest 30 min.	If necessary, turn roast over and defrost 8 min. more.
Family Steak, 1½ inches thick	3 lbs.	About 14 min.	
T-Bone Steak	16 oz.	About 5 min.	
Pork Chops, ½ inch thick (2)	5 oz. each	About 4 min.	
Pork Chops, ½ inch thick (8)	5 oz. each	About 17 min.	Then remove from package separating chops. Defrost 8 to 10 minutes more.
Poultry			
Chicken, Roasting	5¾ lbs.	17 min. breast side up; rest 10 min.; about 17 min., breast side down.	Rest 10 minutes more. Then remove neck and giblets and rinse under cool water.
Chicken, Fryer (cut-up)	2¾ lbs.	12 min. in package; remove from package; 7 min. in single layer.	After first defrost period, remove chicken from package and separate into single layer.
Chicken, Drumsticks (5)	1 lb. each	About 6 min.	
Cornish Game Hens (1)	1¼ lbs.	About 9 min.	Then let rest 10 minutes before removing neck and giblets.
Cornish Game Hens (2)	1¼ lbs. each	About 17 min.	Then let rest 10 minutes before removing neck and giblets.
Turkey, Whole	12 lbs.	20 min. one side; 20 min. other side; 15 min. breast down; 15 min. breast up; remove from back; 12 min. more.	Defrost in bag until near end. After defrost times, let rest 10 minutes. Then remove neck and giblets and rinse under cool water.
Turkey, Boneless Roast	2 lbs.	12 min.	Rest 5 minutes. If necessary, turn over and defrost 5 minutes more.
	2¾ lbs.	17 min.	Rest 5 minutes. If necessary, turn over and defrost 7 minutes more.
	3¾ lbs.	20 min.	Rest 5 minutes. If necessary, turn over and defrost 7 minutes more.
Fish and Seafood			
Fish, Fillets	1 lb.	4 min.; turn over; about 4 min. more.	Defrost in package. Then open package and separate fillets to allow to finish defrosting.
Lobster Tail	8 oz.	About 4 min.	

Reheating Guide

Refrigerated and Frozen Prepared Foods

This page includes some of the more frequently used refrigerated and frozen foods that can be easily heated in the microwave oven. The defrost feature allows the foods to heat without constant watching or stirring, and eliminates the possibility of overcooking the edges.

If you don't see a specific food in the list, look for a similar type food. Use the refrigerated food times as a guide for reheating leftovers, make-ahead dishes, or take-out foods that you've stored in the refrigerator. Use the frozen food times as a guide to commercially frozen foods or ones you freeze yourself.

It is important, where possible, to stir the foods once toward the end of the heating time. If it is a food that should not be stirred, allow the food to stand several minutes before serving. This will give the heat at the edges time to reach the center.

Most foods should be reheated in some type of covered dish. Wax paper, a casserole cover or an overturned plate make a good covering. If using plastic wrap, pierce it so the steam can escape. For sandwich and bread items, wrap in a napkin or paper towel.

	REFRIGERATED				FROZEN			
FOOD	Amount	Time (Minutes)	Amount	Time (Minutes)	Amount	Time (Minutes)	Amount	Time (Minutes)
Vegetables & Side Dishes								
Cooked Vegetables	1 cup	DEFROST 7	3 cups	DEFROST 10	1 cup	DEFROST 7 HIGH 1½	3 cups	DEFROST 12 HIGH 8
Mashed Potatoes	1 cup	DEFROST 5	2 cups	DEFROST 10	1 cup	DEFROST 12	2 cups	DEFROST 17 HIGH 6
Baked Beans	1 cup	DEFROST 5	4 cups	DEFROST 17	1 cup	DEFROST 5 HIGH 3	4 cups	DEFROST 12 HIGH 5
Cooked Rice	1 cup	DEFROST 4	4 cups	DEFROST 14	1 cup	DEFROST 5 HIGH 1½	4 cups	DEFROST 10 HIGH 6
Cooked Noodles	1 cup	DEFROST 5	2 cups	DEFROST 14	1 cup	DEFROST 7 HIGH 3	2 cups	DEFROST 12 HIGH 8
Sandwiches								
Ham and Cheese Sandwich	1 sand.	DEFROST 2	2 sand.	DEFROST 4	1 sand.	DEFROST 4	2 sand.	DEFROST 7
Hamburgers	1 patty	DEFROST 2	3 patties	DEFROST 5	1 patty	DEFROST 4	3 patties	DEFROST 5
Dinners								
Meat, Potato, Vegetable	1 tray or plate	DEFROST 4-5	2 trays or plates	DEFROST 6-7	1 tray or plate	DEFROST 6-7	2 trays or plates	DEFROST 8-9
Meats								
Fried Chicken	1 piece	DEFROST 4	6 pieces	DEFROST 7	1 piece	DEFROST 2 HIGH 2	6 pieces	DEFROST 7 HIGH 5
Sliced Ham	1 slice	DEFROST 2	4 slices	DEFROST 12	1 slice	DEFROST 4	4 slices	DEFROST 7 HIGH 2
Sliced Pork	1 slice	DEFROST 4	4 slices	DEFROST 12	1 slice	DEFROST 4	4 slices	DEFROST 7 HIGH 6
Main Dishes								
Beef Stroganoff	1 cup	DEFROST 7	4 cups	DEFROST 17 HIGH 1½	1 cup	DEFROST 7 HIGH 5	4 cups	DEFROST 19 HIGH 8
Lasagne	1 serving	DEFROST 7	8 x 8 (6 servings)	DEFROST 17 HIGH 14	1 serving	DEFROST 10 HIGH 7	8 x 8 (6 servings)	DEFROST 29 HIGH 15 DEFROST 12 HIGH 3
Spaghetti Sauce	1 cup	DEFROST 7	4 cups	DEFROST 17 HIGH 5	1 cup	DEFROST 7 HIGH 3	4 cups	DEFROST 17 HIGH 20
Chili	1 cup	DEFROST 7	4 cups	DEFROST 17 HIGH 3	1 cup	DEFROST 7 HIGH 3	4 cups	DEFROST 17 HIGH 14
Enchilladas	2 enchilladas	DEFROST 7	8 x 8 (6 servings)	DEFROST 17 HIGH 9	4 enchilladas	DEFROST 14 HIGH 5	8 x 8 (6 servings)	DEFROST 24 HIGH 15
Sweet & Sour Pork	1 cup	DEFROST 7	4 cups	DEFROST 17	1 cup	DEFROST 7 HIGH 5	4 cups	DEFROST 19 HIGH 8
Turkey-Noodle Casserole	1 cup	DEFROST 5	4 cups	DEFROST 22	1 cup	DEFROST 7 HIGH 5	4 cups	DEFROST 24 HIGH 12
Macaroni & Cheese	1 cup	DEFROST 7	4 cups	DEFROST 17 HIGH 8	1 cup	DEFROST 7 HIGH 5	4 cups	DEFROST 24 HIGH 12

Meats and Casseroles

Less tender meats like this pot roast need long slow cooking to become tender. The Defrost feature works nicely for this purpose.

SAUCY POT ROAST

3 to 4-lb. pot roast,	**1 can (10¾ oz.) condensed**
1½ inches thick	**cream of mushroom soup**
1 envelope onion soup mix	**¼ cup water**

Place roast in 3-quart casserole. Sprinkle with soup mix. Spoon mushroom soup over top. Add water. Cook HIGH, covered, 10 MINUTES. Then DEFROST 36 MINUTES. Turn meat over. DEFROST 24 MINUTES. Turn meat over and DEFROST 24 MINUTES more, or until tender. Skim fat from sauce and serve sauce with roast.

6 to 8 servings

HIGH SETTING	10 MIN.
DEFROST SETTING	36 MIN.
TURN MEAT	
DEFROST SETTING	24 MIN.
TURN MEAT	
DEFROST SETTING	24 MIN.
TOTAL	1 HOUR, 34 MIN.

Stroganoff can be made with round steak when you use Defrost to slowly simmer the meat.

ROUND STEAK STROGANOFF

2 lbs. round steak, cut into	**3 tablespoons all-purpose flour**
strips	**1 teaspoon dry mustard**
1 pint sliced fresh mushrooms	**½ teaspoon salt**
1 medium onion, sliced	**½ cup water**
3 teaspoons or cubes beef	**½ cup red wine**
bouillon	**½ cup sour cream**

In 2½-quart casserole, combine all ingredients except sour cream. Cook HIGH, covered, 9 MINUTES. Stir meat and then DEFROST 60 to 85 MINUTES, or until meat is tender, stirring occasionally. Stir in sour cream. Serve over cooked rice or noodles.

6 servings

HIGH SETTING	9 MIN.
DEFROST SETTING	85 MIN.
TOTAL	1 HOUR, 34 MIN.

Defrost allows the ham to evenly heat through to the center.

PINEAPPLE GLAZED HAM

1 small ready-to-eat ham
  (2½ to 3½ lbs.)
⅓ cup firmly packed brown
  sugar
⅓ cup drained crushed
  pineapple

1 teaspoon dry mustard
8 to 10 whole cloves,
  if desired

In shallow baking dish, place ham fat side down on roasting rack or inverted saucer. DEFROST, uncovered, 24 MINUTES. Then Cook HIGH 15 MINUTES. Turn ham fat side up; Cook HIGH 15 MINUTES more. Combine brown sugar, pineapple, and mustard. Slash fat at 1-inch intervals and insert cloves in fat. Spoon pineapple mixture over ham. DEFROST 12 MINUTES, or until meat thermometer registers 115° (do not leave thermometer in oven when cooking). Let stand, covered with foil, 20 minutes, or until thermometer registers 130°.

about 8 servings

TIP: Other favorite ham glazes can be substituted for this pineapple glaze.

DEFROST SETTING	24 MIN.
HIGH SETTING	15 MIN.
TURN HAM OVER	
HIGH SETTING	15 MIN.
ADD GLAZE	
DEFROST SETTING	12 MIN.
STAND	20 MIN.
TOTAL	1 HOUR, 26 MIN.

Defrost is ideal for the slow simmering needed when cooking a soup like this.

HAM AND LENTIL SOUP

1 cup dry lentils
1 ham hock (1¼ to 1½ lbs.)
1 medium onion, sliced
1 carrot, sliced

¼ teaspoon pepper
1 tablespoon Worcestershire
  sauce
6 cups water

In 3-quart casserole, combine all ingredients. Cook HIGH, covered, 14 MINUTES, or until mixture just begins to boil. Then DEFROST 70 MINUTES. Remove ham hock from broth and let cool a few minutes. Then cut meat from bone and return meat to soup. If necessary, Cook HIGH 6 to 9 MINUTES to reheat soup.

4 to 5 servings

TIP: For Ham and Split Pea Soup, substitute split peas for the lentils.

HIGH SETTING	14 MIN.
DEFROST SETTING	70 MIN.
STAND	10 MIN.
HIGH SETTING	9 MIN.
TOTAL	1 HOUR, 43 MIN.

Defrost aids the even cooking of this custard-like sandwich.

CHEESE AND SHRIMP BAKE

8 slices bread
1 or 2 cans (4½ oz. each)
  shrimp, drained
½ cup (1 stalk) chopped
  celery
2 tablespoons chopped
  onion
1 can (10¾ oz.) condensed
  cream of mushroom soup

2 tablespoons lemon juice
½ teaspoon Worcestershire
  sauce
4 oz. shredded or sliced
  American, Cheddar, or
  Swiss cheese
¾ cup milk
3 eggs
¼ cup butter or margarine

If desired, trim crusts from bread. (Use crust for dressing or croutons.) Arrange 4 slices of bread on bottom of ungreased 2-quart (8 x 8) baking dish. Top with shrimp, celery, and onion. Combine soup with lemon juice and Worcestershire sauce; spoon over shrimp. Top with cheese and remaining 4 slices of bread. Beat together milk and eggs; pour over sandwich mixture. Cut butter into pieces and place on top. Cover with plastic wrap and refrigerate 6 to 12 hours or overnight.

To cook, loosen plastic wrap slightly and DEFROST 14 MINUTES. Then Cook HIGH about 9 MINUTES, or until hot and bubbly in center.

4 servings

TIP: Tuna fish can be substituted for the shrimp.

(REFRIGERATE	6 to 12 HOURS)
DEFROST SETTING	14 MIN.
HIGH SETTING	9 MIN.
TOTAL	23 MIN.

With regular cooking, a Quiche overcooks at the edge before the center is set. Now Defrost makes it possible to cook it in the microwave oven.

QUICHE LORRAINE

8 slices bacon
9-inch baked pastry shell
3 eggs
1 teaspoon salt
Dash pepper
Dash nutmeg

1 cup milk
⅔ cup (5⅓-fl. oz. can)
  evaporated milk
1½ cups (6 oz.) shredded
  Swiss cheese

Arrange bacon between paper towels on paper plate or baking dish. Cook HIGH about 7 MINUTES or until crisp. Prepare and cook pastry shell conventionally.

Beat together eggs, salt, pepper, and nutmeg. Measure milk into 2- or 4-cup measure. Add evaporated milk. Cook HIGH, uncovered, 5 MINUTES or until hot. Arrange cheese in bottom of pastry shell. Crumble bacon over top. Add hot milk to egg mixture, beat well. Pour into pastry shell.

Cook HIGH, uncovered, 3 MINUTES. Then DEFROST 5 MINUTES. Carefully move cooked outer portion of filling to center. DEFROST 14 MINUTES more, or until knife inserted near center comes out clean. Let stand 10 minutes before cutting into wedges.

5 to 6 servings

BACON ON HIGH	7 MIN.
HEAT MILK	5 MIN.
HIGH SETTING	3 MIN.
DEFROST SETTING	5 MIN.
DEFROST SETTING	14 MIN.
STAND	10 MIN.
TOTAL	44 MIN.

With Defrost you can start with a frozen turkey roast and in about an hour have a juicy, evenly cooked roast.

TURKEY ROAST

3-lb. frozen boneless rolled   **Favorite glaze, if desired**
turkey roast

Place frozen roast skin side down on roasting rack or inverted saucer in 2-quart (8 x 8) baking dish. DEFROST, uncovered, 35 MINUTES. Then Cook HIGH 8 MINUTES. Turn roast skin side up and Cook HIGH 23 MINUTES more, or until meat thermometer registers 180°, brushing with glaze during last 5 minutes (do not leave thermometer in oven when cooking). Let stand 10 minutes or until thermometer registers 195°

8 to 10 servings

DEFROST SETTING	35 MIN.
HIGH SETTING	8 MIN.
TURN	
HIGH SETTING	23 MIN.
STAND	10 MIN.
TOTAL	1 HOUR, 16 MIN.

The Defrost feature is ideal for simmering the chicken and vegetables, but regular cooking is necessary for cooking the dumplings.

CHICKEN AND DUMPLINGS

3-lb. stewing chicken	**Dumplings**
2 stalks celery, cut into	**1½ cups unsifted all-purpose**
1-inch pieces	**flour**
1 medium onion, sliced	**2 teaspoons baking powder**
1 bay leaf	**½ teaspoon salt**
4 peppercorns	**1 teaspoon parsley flakes**
1 tablespoon salt	**⅔ cup milk**
4 cups water	**1 egg**
8 carrots, peeled and sliced	**2 tablespoons oil**
⅓ cup all-purpose flour	
½ cup water	

In 4-quart casserole or Dutch oven, combine chicken, celery, onion, bay leaf, peppercorns, salt, and 4 cups water. Cook HIGH, covered, 10 MINUTES, or until mixture just begins to boil. Then DEFROST 70 MINUTES. Add carrots and DEFROST 20 MINUTES, or until carrots are almost tender. Remove bay leaf.

Combine flour and ½ cup water; stir into chicken mixture. Spoon dumplings by rounded tablespoons onto hot chicken mixture. Cook HIGH, covered, 10 MINUTES, or until dumplings are no longer doughy.

Dumplings: In mixing bowl combine flour, baking powder, salt, and parsley. Combine milk, egg, and oil; add to other ingredients and mix just until moistened (mixture will be soft).

5 to 6 servings

HIGH SETTING	10 MIN.
DEFROST SETTING	70 MIN.
ADD CARROTS	
DEFROST SETTING	20 MIN.
ADD DUMPLINGS	
HIGH SETTING	10 MIN.
TOTAL	1 HOUR, 50 MIN.

Breads and Side Dishes

Defrost is ideal for the slow simmering necessary to cook dry beans and to allow the seasonings to blend with the beans. The microwave oven provides "cool cooking" on a warm day.

LIGHT BAKED BEANS

2 cups dry navy beans
6 cups water
¼ cup firmly packed brown sugar
¼ cup chopped onion
¼ cup chili sauce or catsup

1 tablespoon prepared mustard
2 tablespoons molasses
2 teaspoons salt
2 slices bacon, cut into pieces

Wash beans. Place in 3-quart casserole. Add water; cover and let stand 12 hours or overnight.

Place casserole (with beans and water) in microwave oven and Cook HIGH, covered, 15 MINUTES, or until mixture just begins to boil, then DEFROST 60 MINUTES, or until beans are tender.

Stir in remaining ingredients and continue to DEFROST, covered, 2 HOURS, stirring occasionally and adding a small amount of water if beans become dry.

6 to 8 servings

TIPS: The beans can be eaten after simmering in the sauce about 1 hour, but are more flavorful if allowed to simmer the additional time.

Use the directions for cooking the beans in water as a guide when cooking beans for other uses.

STAND	12 HOURS
HIGH SETTING	15 MIN.
DEFROST SETTING	60 MIN.
ADD SEASONINGS	
DEFROST SETTING	2 HOURS
TOTAL	3 HOURS, 15 MIN.

Since rice needs a certain amount of time to rehydrate, Defrost can save on energy while allowing the mixture to slowly simmer. Since the mixture simmers rather than boils, we have reduced the size of casserole and the amount of liquid.

RICE PILAF

¼ cup butter or margarine
1½ cups rice
½ cup chopped onion
½ cup chopped celery
2 tablespoons parsley flakes

1 can (10½ oz.) condensed chicken broth
¼ teaspoon salt
¼ teaspoon leaf thyme
Dash pepper
1⅓ cups water

In 1½ or 2-quart casserole, combine all ingredients. Cook HIGH, covered, 10 MINUTES, or until mixture starts to boil. Then DEFROST 30 MINUTES, or until rice is tender, stirring occasionally. Let stand a few minutes; fluff with fork.

5 to 6 servings

HIGH SETTING	10 MIN.
DEFROST SETTING	30 MIN.
STAND	3 MIN.
TOTAL	43 MIN.

Wheat germ adds nutritional value along with a brown color to this moist bread. Defrost aids the even cooking of the bread.

WHEAT GERM BREAD

1 cup warm water (about 85°)	2 tablespoons oil
1 package active dry yeast	1 egg
¼ cup firmly packed brown sugar	½ cup wheat germ
1½ teaspoons salt	about 2½ cups unsifted all-purpose flour

In large mixing bowl, combine warm water and yeast. Stir in brown sugar, salt, oil, egg, wheat germ, and 1½ cups flour. Beat about 3 minutes. Stir in remaining flour to form a stiff batter. Cover; let rise in warm place until light and doubled in size, about 1½ hours.

Stir down batter. Spread in ungreased 1½-quart (8 x 4) loaf dish. Cover; let rise in warm place until doubled, about 45 minutes. DEFROST, uncovered, 7 MINUTES. Then Cook HIGH 5 to 6 MINUTES, or until no doughy spots remain. Cool 5 minutes. Loosen edges and turn out of dish. Cool.

1 loaf

TIP: For a warm place to let bread rise, bring a cup of water to boil in microwave oven (about 5 min.). Turn off oven, leaving boiling water in oven, place bread dough in oven (covering is not necessary because of moisture from water). If oven becomes cool, remove bread and bring water to a boil again.

RISE IN BOWL	1½ HOURS
RISE IN BAKING DISH	45 MIN.
DEFROST SETTING	7 MIN.
HIGH SETTING	6 MIN.
TOTAL	2 HOURS, 28 MIN.

Here Defrost slowly heats the bread throughout, so it cooks quickly and evenly.

ENGLISH MUFFIN BREAD

5 cups unsifted all-purpose flour	2 teaspoons salt
2 packages active dry yeast	2½ cups milk
1 tablespoon sugar	1 tablespoon warm water
	¼ teaspoon baking soda

In large mixing bowl, combine 3 cups flour, yeast, sugar, and salt. In 4-cup measure, heat milk until warm, about 2 minutes; add to flour mixture. Beat by hand or with mixer until smooth. Stir in remaining flour to form a stiff batter. Cover; let rise in warm place until light and doubled in size, about 1 hour.

Combine water and baking soda. Stir down yeast batter; blend in soda mixture, mixing until well blended. Divided batter between 2 ungreased 1½-quart (8 x 4) loaf dishes. Cover and let rise in warm place until doubled, about 45 minutes.

Place loaves, one at a time, in microwave oven and DEFROST, uncovered, 7 MINUTES. Then Cook HIGH 5 to 6 MINUTES, or until no doughy spots remain. Cool 5 minutes; loosen edges and turn out of dish. Cool completely. To serve, slice and toast in toaster or under broiler until edges are brown.

2 loaves

RISE IN BOWL	1 HOUR
RISE IN BAKING DISHES	45 MIN.
EACH LOAF:	
DEFROST SETTING	7 MIN.
HIGH SETTING	6 MIN.
TOTAL	1 HOUR, 58 MIN.

The extra water in the oven keeps the bread moist and the oven warm. Defrost is turned on every 15 minutes to thaw and warm the dough.

THAWING AND PROOFING FROZEN BREAD DOUGH

Heat 4 cups of water in a 4-cup measure until steaming hot (12 min.). Place frozen loaf in greased 1½-quart (8 x 4) loaf dish. Place, uncovered, in oven with the water, DEFROST 3 MINUTES. Turn off oven. Let stand 15 minutes. Repeat defrost and stand sequence 3 to 4 more times or until dough is just above top of pan. Bake as directed on package.

WATER ON HIGH	12 MIN.
DEFROST SETTING	3 MIN.
STAND	15 MIN.
DEFROST SETTING	3 MIN.
STAND	15 MIN.
DEFROST SETTING	3 MIN.
STAND	15 MIN.
DEFROST SETTING	3 MIN.
STAND	15 MIN.
TOTAL	1 HOUR, 24 MIN.

TIP: The frozen dough is best baked conventionally. It tends to become tough when cooked with microwaves.

Desserts

Defrost allows more area of the pastry shell to lightly brown without starting to overcook.

BAKED PASTRY SHELL

Prepare pie crust stick or enough mix for one-crust pie as directed on package. Roll out and fit into 9-inch pie plate. Flute edge and prick bottom and sides with fork. DEFROST, uncovered, 5 MINUTES. Then Cook HIGH 3 to 5 MINUTES, or until crust is bubbly and brown spots begin to appear.

9-inch baked pastry shell

TIP: The pie crust mix and sticks have a yellow color that makes a nice golden color when cooked. If you use a home recipe, you can achieve a yellow color by adding about 4 drops yellow food color to the water.

DEFROST SETTING	5 MIN.
HIGH SETTING	5 MIN.
TOTAL	10 MIN.

The slow cooking necessary for Pecan Pie is another good use of Defrost.

PECAN PIE

9-inch baked pastry shell
3 eggs, slightly beaten
1 cup dark corn syrup
¼ cup firmly packed
   brown sugar

½ tablespoon all-purpose flour
1 teaspoon vanilla
¾ cup chopped pecans
3 tablespoons butter or
   margarine, melted

Prepare and cook pastry shell as directed above. Combine remaining ingredients. Pour into cooked pastry shell. DEFROST, uncovered, 20 MINUTES, or until knife inserted near center comes out clean. Cool.

9-inch pie

PASTRY	
DEFROST SETTING	5 MIN.
HIGH SETTING	5 MIN.
FILLING	
DEFROST SETTING	20 MIN.
TOTAL	30 MIN.

For creamy old-fashioned bread pudding, we cooked it in a dish of hot water and used Defrost.

BREAD PUDDING

2 cups soft bread cubes	½ cup raisins
2 cups milk	1 teaspoon vanilla
2 eggs, slightly beaten	⅛ teaspoon salt
⅓ cup sugar	Cinnamon

Place bread in 1-quart shallow casserole and Cook HIGH, uncovered, 3 MINUTES to dry bread. Measure milk into 2- or 4-cup glass measure. Cook HIGH, uncovered, 4 MINUTES, or until hot. Combine remaining ingredients except cinnamon. Mix in hot milk. Add to bread in casserole, mixing well. Sprinkle with cinnamon.

Set in baking dish with about 1 inch hot water. Cook HIGH, uncovered, 2 MINUTES. Then DEFROST 10 MINUTES. Stir. Continue to DEFROST 7 MINUTES, or until knife inserted near center comes out clean.

5 to 6 servings

BREAD CUBES ON	
HIGH	3 MIN.
MILK ON HIGH	4 MIN.
HIGH SETTING	2 MIN.
DEFROST SETTING	10 MIN.
STIR	
DEFROST SETTING	7 MIN.
TOTAL	26 MIN.

Defrost allows this custard to cook slowly, forming a creamy, smooth finished pudding.

SWEDISH RICE PUDDING

2 cups milk	¼ teaspoon cinnamon
2 eggs, slightly beaten	½ cup quick-cooking rice
½ cup sugar	½ cup raisins
1 teaspoon vanilla	

Measure milk into 2- or 4-cup glass measure. Cook HIGH, uncovered, 4 MINUTES or until hot. In 1½-quart casserole, combine eggs, sugar, vanilla, and cinnamon, mixing well. Mix in rice, raisins, and hot milk.

Set in baking dish with about 1 inch hot water. Cook HIGH, uncovered, 3 MINUTES. Then DEFROST 10 MINUTES. Stir to move cooked portion to center. Continue to DEFROST 10 MINUTES, or until knife inserted near center comes out clean.

5 to 6 servings

MILK ON HIGH	4 MIN.
HIGH SETTING	3 MIN.
DEFROST SETTING	10 MIN.
STIR	
DEFROST SETTING	10 MIN.
TOTAL	27 MIN.

Without Defrost, this type of cheesecake would overcook around the edge before the center is set. A cake dish is substituted for the traditional metal springform pan.

DELUXE CHEESECAKE

Crust
- ½ cup unsifted all-purpose flour
- 1 tablespoon sugar
- ¼ teaspoon baking powder
- ⅛ teaspoon salt
- 3 tablespoons butter or margarine
- 1 to 2 tablespoons milk

Filling
- 2 packages (8 oz. each) cream cheese
- ¾ cup sugar
- 1½ tablespoons all-purpose flour
- 1 tablespoon lemon juice
- 2 tablespoons cream
- ⅛ teaspoon salt
- ½ teaspoon vanilla
- 3 eggs

For crust, combine flour, sugar, baking powder, and salt. Cut in butter until particles are fine. Sprinkle milk over mixture, stirring with fork until moist enough to hold together. Form into a ball. Press mixture evenly on bottom and up sides of 1½-quart (8-inch round) baking dish. Cook HIGH, uncovered, 5 MINUTES, or until brown spots just begin to appear.

For filling, soften cream cheese (1½ min.); beat on medium speed of mixer until creamy. Beat in remaining ingredients, adding eggs one at a time. Pour into cooked crust. DEFROST, uncovered, 20 MINUTES, or until filling is almost set.

Cool and refrigerate several hours before serving.

10 to 12 servings.

CRUST ON HIGH	5 MIN.
DEFROST SETTING	20 MIN.
TOTAL	25 MIN.

Cheesecake needs slow cooking for a creamy texture. Defrost makes it simple to do.

CREAMY CHEESECAKE

Crust
- ¼ cup butter or margarine
- 12 graham cracker squares, crushed (⅔ cup crumbs)
- 2 tablespoons all-purpose flour
- 2 tablespoons sugar
- ¼ teaspoon cinnamon

Filling
- 1 package (8 oz.) cream cheese
- ⅓ cup sugar
- 1 egg
- 1 tablespoon lemon juice

Topping
- 1 cup sour cream
- 3 tablespoons sugar
- ½ teaspoon almond or vanilla extract

For crust, melt butter in 1½-quart (8-inch round) baking dish (30 sec.). Mix in remaining Crust ingredients and press mixture on bottom and halfway up sides of dish.

For filling, soften cream cheese (45 sec.); beat with remaining Filling ingredients. Pour into crust and DEFROST, uncovered, 7 MINUTES.

For topping, combine Topping ingredients. Spread over partially cooked filling. DEFROST, uncovered 5 MINUTES, or until set. Chill several hours or overnight.

6 to 8 servings

DEFROST SETTING	7 MIN.
ADD TOPPING	
DEFROST SETTING	5 MIN.
TOTAL	12 MIN.

This moist date cake has an attractive topping of chocolate pieces and chopped nuts. Use the timing as a guide for cooking similar "scratch" cake recipes.

CHOCO-DATE CAKE

¾ cup butter or margarine
1 cup sugar
2 eggs
1¾ cups unsifted all-purpose
   flour
1 tablespoon unsweetened
   cocoa
¾ teaspoon baking soda

½ teaspoon salt
1 teaspoon vanilla
¾ cup water
1 cup chopped dates
1 cup (6-oz. pkg.) semisweet
   chocolate pieces
½ cup chopped nuts

In large mixing bowl, soften butter (45 sec.). Beat in sugar and eggs. Add flour, cocoa, soda, salt, vanilla, water, and dates. Stir until combined. Spread in ungreased 2-quart (8 x 8) baking dish. Sprinkle with chocolate pieces and nuts. DEFROST, uncovered, 10 MINUTES. Then Cook HIGH 10 MINUTES, or until toothpick inserted in center comes out clean.

8- x 8-inch cake

DEFROST SETTING	10 MIN.
HIGH SETTING	10 MIN.
TOTAL	20 MIN.

Carrots in the cake and a butter-orange sauce make this cake double moist and double good.

HONEY 'N SPICE CARROT CAKE

2 eggs
2 medium carrots, cut
   into pieces
½ cup butter or margarine,
   softened
½ cup honey
½ teaspoon vanilla
1 cup unsifted all-purpose
   flour
½ teaspoon baking soda
½ teaspoon salt

½ teaspoon cinnamon
½ teaspoon nutmeg
½ cup chopped nuts

Sauce
¼ cup orange juice
¼ cup honey
¼ cup butter or margarine
1 to 2 tablespoons orange
   liqueur, if desired

In blender, process eggs and carrots at medium speed until carrots are in fine pieces. In bowl, soften butter (30 sec.). Blend in honey and vanilla. Beat in carrot mixture. Stir in flour, soda, salt, cinnamon, nutmeg, and nuts. Spread evenly in ungreased 1½-quart (8 x 4) baking dish.

DEFROST, uncovered, 8 MINUTES. Then Cook HIGH 5 to 6 MINUTES, or until toothpick inserted in center comes out clean. Pierce cake at ½-inch intervals with toothpick or long-tined fork. For sauce, combine orange juice, honey, and butter in 2-cup measure. Cook HIGH, uncovered, 2 to 3 MINUTES, or until mixture boils. Stir in liqueur. Pour warm sauce over cake. Cool. If desired, serve with whipped cream.

8 x 4-inch cake

TIP: If you don't have a blender, grate the carrot before adding it to the butter-egg mixture.

CAKE:	
DEFROST SETTING	8 MIN.
HIGH SETTING	6 MIN.
SAUCE:	
HIGH SETTING	3 MIN.
TOTAL	17 MIN.

Defrost helps melt the chocolate for the frosting and aids the even cooking of these bars.

CRUNCHY TOFFEE BARS

⅔ cup butter or margarine
1 cup firmly packed brown
   sugar
½ cup light corn syrup
1 teaspoon salt
1 teaspoon vanilla

3 cups quick or old-fashioned
   rolled oats
2 cups granola cereal
1 cup (6-oz. pkg.) semisweet
   chocolate pieces
½ cup peanut butter

In 2-quart (8 x 8) baking dish, melt butter (1½ min.). Blend in brown sugar, corn syrup, salt, and vanilla. Stir in rolled oats and granola until evenly mixed. Pat evenly in baking dish. DEFROST, uncovered, 10 MINUTES. Then Cook HIGH 5 MINUTES, or until bubbly throughout. Cool slightly.

Melt chocolate by placing in mixing bowl and DEFROST, uncovered, 4 MINUTES, or until chocolate is softened. Stir in peanut butter. Spread on bars. Refrigerate to set frosting. Cut into bars.

About 48 bars

BARS:	
DEFROST SETTING	10 MIN.
HIGH SETTING	5 MIN.
FROSTING:	
DEFROST SETTING	4 MIN.
TOTAL	19 MIN.

Dream Bars contain a high concentration of sugar, so there may be a tendency to overcook in certain areas. The use of Defrost helps assure even cooking.

DREAM BARS

½ cup butter or margarine
½ cup firmly packed brown
   sugar
1¼ cups unsifted all-purpose
   flour
2 eggs
1 cup firmly packed brown
   sugar

2 tablespoons all-purpose flour
¼ teaspoon baking powder
¼ teaspoon salt
1 teaspoon vanilla
1½ cups flaked or shredded
   coconut
½ cup chopped nuts

In mixing bowl, soften butter (30 sec.). Blend in brown sugar and flour until well mixed. Pat evenly in 2-quart (8 x 8) baking dish. Cook HIGH, uncovered, 5 MINUTES, or until brown spots just begin to appear.

Beat eggs slightly. Stir in remaining ingredients. Spoon mixture over crust, spreading to edges. DEFROST, uncovered, 6 MINUTES. Then Cook HIGH 6 MINUTES more, or until topping is puffed and set.

About 48 bars

HIGH SETTING	5 MIN.
DEFROST SETTING	6 MIN.
HIGH SETTING	6 MIN.
TOTAL	17 MIN.

The Miracle of Microwave Cookery

The rewards of microwave cooking are many and varied. To begin with, there is speed. Have you ever before baked a potato in five minutes, cooked a family-size roast in eighteen to thirty minutes, had a casserole on the table in six minutes, baked a custard in three minutes? And then there's comfort. No longer need you plan hot-weather meals that must be cooked on top of the stove to avoid the heat of a conventional oven.

To top all this off, the microwave oven is incredibly easy to use. It can make true do-it-yourselfers out of dad and the children, leaving you free at any mealtime when there's something else you'd rather be doing. It is, indeed, the piece of kitchen equipment that the home cook has long been waiting for.

While you and your oven are new to one another, rely on the times given in the recipes; but as you become more familiar with microwave cooking, you'll learn to judge easily the degree of doneness of any food. Take cakes as an example. As you know, a cake is done when it begins to shrink away from the sides of the pan. This is also true of a microwave-baked cake—but, unlike a cake baked conventionally, its top will still be very moist. You will learn that when you remove the cake from the oven and let it stand, the top will finish cooking and dry. During baking, cakes (and some other baked dishes, as well) must be rotated—turned 90°—one or more times to ensure even cooking. See individual recipes.

While most owners of microwave ovens value them for their speed, it's true that this new-day appliance does some kinds of cooking in a manner far superior to the conventional way. Rice, for example, cooks like magic—just measure rice and water into a casserole, stir once during cooking time, and the rice will turn out beautifully fluffy, of just the right consistency. And the casserole dish is easy to clean up.

White or cream sauces and milk puddings are another better-than-any-other-way category, for when you cook these in a microwave oven there's no tedious, constant stirring as there is when you cook them on top of the stove. Once the ingredients are mixed in the cooking dish, they can be placed in the microwave oven, stirred once or twice, and they come out beautifully smooth, of just the right thickness. There is never any danger of burning the food. And, once again, the cooking dish is easily cleaned.

OPPOSITE: *Many kinds of dishes—but nothing metal—can be used in the microwave oven.*

Besides doing many kinds of cooking for you well and speedily, the microwave oven takes over a lot of small, picky kitchen jobs and does them better than they can be accomplished in any other way. Melting butter, for example: butter melts in seconds in your microwave oven and you needn't fear that it will be browned. (Cover butter with a loose piece of plastic wrap to avoid spatters and boilover.) The same is true of melting chocolate: in your microwave oven chocolate melts quickly and easily, with no risk of scorching. Even so simple a thing as making yourself a cup of instant coffee becomes simpler, for water boils in virtually no time in a glass measuring cup in your microwave oven. Rolls warm almost instantly. Day-old baked goods come from the microwave oven tasting and smelling as if they had been freshly baked.

Virtually instant parties can be conjured up out of your microwave oven. Appetizers, either made from scratch or pre-prepared and frozen, can go from the microwave oven to the waiting party guests in practically no time at all.

There's a bonus at clean-up time, too. Many recipes in this book, you will see, call for disposables—for cooking on paper towels or paper plates, or for using plastic wrap or waxed paper as covers. Paper cups also come into service. Even when you use more conventional dishes, such as glass or pottery casseroles, you will find that they are exceptionally easy to wash, without the stubborn burned-on bits that so often result from conventional cooking.

When in doubt about the size of casserole dish to be used, in trying your own recipes, choose the larger rather than the smaller one, especially if the recipe calls for milk. That way you'll have no boilovers, which are messy to clean up and easily avoidable if you choose a cooking dish of ample size.

Can you prepare a whole meal—other than uncooked foods, of course—in your microwave oven? Indeed you can. Here is a suggested family dinner:

Spring Pea Soup (page 28)
Beef Goulash (page 34)   Heated Hard Rolls
Tossed Green Salad
Apple Betty (page 150)   Instant Coffee (page 127)

Make the apple betty first, and let it stand while you cook the goulash. While that cooks, prepare the salad. Now cook the soup, letting the goulash stand. The hard rolls heat in a matter of seconds. Make coffee, and dinner is served.

Now you're ready for guests. For dinner, serve:

Cheddar Cheese Canapés (page 14)   Cooked Shrimp (page 19) with Dip
Cream Sudanese (page 22)
Rolled Ribs of Beef (page 30)   Green Beans Piquant (page 96)
Cauliflower and Tomatoes (page 105)
Lettuce Wedge with Bleu Cheese Dressing
Vanilla Mousse with Strawberry Sauce (page 146)   Demitasse

Cook the shrimp and make the dessert in the morning so that they have time to chill. Prepare the salad and its dressing before the guests arrive. Make the cheddar cheese canapés just before you serve them in the living room, along with the shrimp, with drinks. The beef cooks while this is going on, is taken from the oven and stands to finish cooking while you cook the vegetables. The coffee, of course, takes only a minute.

With a microwave oven, even a Sunday brunch party can be the fun it should be, instead of a hassle. Offer your guests:

Mulled Pineapple Juice (page 124)
Eggs Benedict (page 82)   Sautéed Mushrooms (page 106)
Sticky Buns (page 138)   Café au Lait (page 127)

Make the sticky buns first, then prepare and serve the pineapple juice. While guests chat and drink juice, make the eggs benedict and the mushrooms. Coffee is the work of a moment, and you're ready to serve.

As you become more familiar with your microwave oven, you'll find yourself organizing and serving many microwave meals, of excellent variety and delectable taste, from plans like these.

A final word: cooking times can vary slightly with house voltage, brand, variety, or season of food product. Use the minimum recommended time, then adjust with 30-second additional heatings, if necessary. Take good care of your microwave oven and it will serve you long and well. Keep it clean (cleanup is very easy) according to your use-and-care booklet. And if you need service, call a trained, competent Sears serviceman, and give him the model number of your microwave oven.

Appetizers

Appetizers, prepared days or weeks before and frozen, can be served piping hot in minutes with the aid of the microwave oven. Canapés with a bread or cracker base should be assembled just before warming to prevent sogginess. Place canapés on a tray or platter with an underliner of paper towels or paper napkins to absorb any moisture. If you are heating a large number of canapes, discard the paper underliner and place heated canapes on a serving plate—not merely for the sake of attractive service but also to keep the canapés from resting on a damp surface.

The microwave oven is ideal for dips and dunks of all kinds—they can be prepared long in advance, placed in serving bowls, and heated in the serving dish with no fuss or bother.

Geri's Sweet and Sour Hot Dogs

6 to 8 servings

2 tablespoons prepared mustard

¼ cup grape jelly

½ pound frankfurters

1 teaspoon butter or margarine, melted

1. Combine mustard and jelly in a 1-cup measuring cup.
2. Cook, covered with plastic wrap, for 2½ minutes.
3. Cut each frankfurter diagonally in 9 to 10 slices. Put in a 1-quart baking dish with butter.
4. Cook, covered, for about 3 minutes.
5. Pour grape jelly sauce over frankfurters. Cook, covered, for 4 minutes.
6. Let stand 2 minutes.
7. Serve hot; use toothpicks to pick up individual slices.

Cocktail Wieners

6 to 8 servings

¼ cup minced onion

2 teaspoons butter

½ cup catsup

1 tablespoon vinegar

½ teaspoon Worcestershire sauce

2 tablespoons brown sugar

½ teaspoon salt

½ teaspoon dry mustard

½ teaspoon paprika

2 to 3 dozen cocktail wieners

1. Combine onion and butter in a 1- to 1½-quart casserole.
2. Cook, covered, for 4 to 5 minutes, or until onion is soft.
3. Add ¼ cup water and stir in remaining ingredients except cocktail wieners.
4. Cook, covered, for 4 to 5 minutes, or until sauce is bubbly.
5. Stir in cocktail wieners.
6. Cook, covered, for about 4 minutes, or until wieners are hot.
7. Let stand, covered, for 2 minutes.
8. Serve warm; use toothpicks to spear individual wieners.

Cheddar Cheese Canapés

24 canapés

¼ cup grated Cheddar cheese

2 tablespoons cream

1 tablespoon grated Parmesan cheese

⅛ teaspoon Worcestershire sauce

⅛ teaspoon hot-pepper sauce

1 tablespoon sesame seeds

24 rounds of toast or crisp crackers

Chopped parsley

1. Combine Cheddar cheese, cream, Parmesan cheese, Worcestershire, hot-pepper sauce, and sesame seeds. Blend with an electric mixer until smooth.
2. Spread 1 teaspoon of the mixture on each of the toast rounds or crackers.
3. Arrange on a platter lined with paper towels.
4. Cook for 20 to 30 seconds, or just until mixture is warm and cheese is melted.
5. Garnish with parsley; serve warm.

Cheese Devils

6 servings

2 cups shredded sharp Cheddar cheese
¼ cup soft butter or margarine
¼ teaspoon dry mustard
Dash of cayenne

1 teaspoon onion juice
1 tablespoon chili sauce
6 slices white bread, toasted

1. Combine all ingredients except toast.
2. Place each toast slice on a paper plate. Divide mixture among toast slices.
3. Cook one at a time, for 2 to 2½ minutes, or until cheese is melted.

Mushroom-Egg Canapés

18 canapés

2 tablespoons butter or margarine
1 tablespoon finely minced onion
½ cup finely chopped mushrooms
2 hard-cooked eggs, finely chopped

1 tablespoon chopped parsley
½ teaspoon salt
18 toast rounds or crackers
¼ cup grated Cheddar cheese

1. Put butter, onion, and mushrooms in a small mixing bowl. Cook, uncovered, for 4 to 5 minutes, or just until mushrooms are soft.
2. Stir in eggs, parsley, and salt.
3. Spread 1 rounded teaspoon of mixture on each toast round. Sprinkle with grated Cheddar cheese.
4. Arrange on a tray lined with paper towels.
5. Cook for about 45 seconds, or just long enough to melt the cheese.
6. Serve warm.

Shrimp Dip

2 cups

1 can (10½ ounces) cream of shrimp soup, undiluted
1 package (8 ounces) cream cheese, softened

1 teaspoon lemon juice
Dash of paprika
Dash of garlic powder

1. Pour soup into a small mixing bowl.
2. Cook, covered, for about 3 minutes, or until hot. Stir well.
3. Beat in cream cheese, lemon juice, paprika, and garlic powder.
4. Keep warm over a candle warmer. Serve as a dip with crisp vegetables.

FOLLOWING PAGES: Left, *Bean Dip, page 19; Cocktail Wieners, page 14; Hot Mexican Cheese Dip, page 20;* right, *Cocktail Shrimp, page 19; Meatball Appetizers, page 20; Shrimp Dip, page 15.*

Crab Meat Supreme

6 servings

¾ pound fresh cooked or canned
   crab meat
½ cup chopped celery
3½ tablespoons mayonnaise
½ teaspoon curry powder

Salt and pepper to taste
6 corn toaster muffins
½ cup potato chip crumbs
6 slices Swiss cheese

1. Pick over crab meat and mix with celery.
2. Stir together mayonnaise and curry powder; mix with crab. Season to taste with salt and pepper.
3. Place each toaster muffin on a paper plate. Pile crab mixture onto muffins. Sprinkle with crumbs; top with a slice of cheese.
4. Cook one at a time, for 2 to 2½ minutes, or until cheese is melted.

Shrimp Olive Dip

about 2½ cups

1 can (10½ ounces) cream of shrimp
   soup, undiluted
1 package (8 ounces) cream cheese,
   cut into chunks
1 can (8 ounces) chopped ripe olives,
   drained

2 tablespoons lemon juice
1 teaspoon Worcestershire sauce
¾ teaspoon curry powder
   (optional)

1. Combine soup and cream cheese in a 1-quart casserole.
2. Cook, covered, for 4 minutes.
3. Remove and stir until cheese is well blended. Stir in remaining ingredients.
4. Cook, covered, for 2 to 3 minutes, or until piping hot.
5. Place over a candle warmer to keep hot and serve as a dip with corn chips or potato chips.

Stuffed Mushrooms

makes 8 to 10

8 to 10 medium mushrooms
2 tablespoons minced onion
3 tablespoons butter or margarine

½ cup dry bread crumbs
¼ teaspoon hot-pepper sauce
2 tablespoons sherry

1. Wipe mushrooms with a damp paper towel. Carefully twist off stems from mushroom caps, leaving caps intact. Chop stems very fine. Place in a small mixing bowl with onion and butter. Cook, uncovered, for 4 to 5 minutes, or until onion is tender.
2. Combine mushroom mixture with bread crumbs, hot-pepper sauce, and sherry and mix well. Fill mushroom caps with this stuffing. Place filled mushrooms in an 8-inch baking dish.
3. Cook, covered, for 4 to 5 minutes, or until mushrooms are piping hot.

Tantalizer Spread

¾ cup

3 strips bacon
1 small tomato, peeled and quartered
1 teaspoon prepared mustard
1 package (3 ounces) cream cheese, cut into cubes

¼ teaspoon celery salt
½ cup blanched almonds

1. Place paper towels in bottom of an 8-inch square dish. Place bacon strips on towels. Cover loosely with another paper towel.
2. Cook for about 5 minutes, or until bacon is very crisp.
3. Put tomato, mustard, cream cheese, and celery salt in blender container. Cover and process until mixture is smooth. Add almonds and bacon and process only until almonds are chopped.
4. Serve with an assortment of crackers.

Bean Dip

3 cups

1 can (1 pound) baked or kidney beans
1 jar (8 ounces) pasteurized process cheese spread

¼ cup catsup
1 teaspoon chili powder
Dash of hot-pepper sauce

1. Pour beans into a 1½-quart casserole. Mash beans with a fork. Add remaining ingredients and blend well.
2. Cook, covered, for 3 to 4 minutes. Stir well.
3. Cook again, covered, for 3 to 4 minutes, or until piping hot.
4. Keep hot on a heated tray or a candle warmer.

Cocktail Shrimp

2 to 3 servings

½ pound raw shrimp
2 tablespoons butter

½ clove garlic, minced
3 tablespoons dry white wine

1. Remove shells and veins from shrimp. Rinse in cold water.
2. Place butter, garlic, and white wine in an 8-inch baking dish or shallow casserole.
3. Cook for 3 minutes.
4. Stir mixture and place shrimp in dish, without stirring. Cover loosely with a piece of waxed paper. Cook for 2 minutes.
5. Stir shrimp, cover, and cook for 1½ minutes or until shrimp are pink in color and just tender. Do not overcook or shrimp will be tough.
6. Pour shrimp and sauce into a small bowl. Season with salt.
7. Chill and serve as an appetizer with desired dunking sauce.

Hot Mexican Cheese Dip

2½ cups

1 pound process American cheese, grated

1 can (10 ounces) green chilies and tomatoes

1. Combine cheese and chilies in a 1½-quart casserole.
2. Cook, covered, for 3 to 4 minutes. Stir thoroughly.
3. Cover and cook again for 3 to 4 minutes.
4. Keep hot on a heated tray or candle warmer and serve with corn chips or potato chips or with crisp raw vegetables.

Deviled Toasties

30 to 35 canapés

½ pound lean ground round steak

2 tablespoons minced onion

1 teaspoon catsup

½ teaspoon prepared mustard

⅛ teaspoon prepared horseradish

1 loaf party rye bread

1. Combine meat, onion, catsup, mustard, and horseradish. Blend well. Put about 1 teaspoon of the mixture on the top of each little slice of bread.
2. Cook, uncovered, 9 at a time on paper towel, for about 4 minutes, or to the desired degree of doneness. Remove to serving plate immediately.

Meatball Appetizers

about 72

1 pound ground beef

½ pound ground pork

1 small onion, finely minced

1 cup milk

1 egg, lightly beaten

1 cup dry bread crumbs

1 teaspoon salt

¼ teaspoon pepper

¼ teaspoon ground allspice

1. Combine ingredients in a large mixing bowl and blend well. Form into small balls, about 1 inch in diameter.
2. Arrange half of the meatballs in a single layer in an oblong baking dish.
3. Cook, uncovered, for 4½ minutes. Turn meatballs over and rearrange so that meatballs on the outer edges are moved into center of baking dish.
4. Continue cooking for 1½ minutes, or until meat loses its red color and meatballs are cooked.
5. Place in a chafing dish to keep hot.
6. Cook remaining meatballs.
7. Serve hot with toothpicks and favorite dunking sauce, if desired.

Soups

Soup any time of the day is a snap with the help of the microwave oven. Prepared soups can be heated right in the serving bowls—great for quick service, and never a pot to wash. Soup combinations and simple chowders are fun and easy to make, and a fine way to use up leftovers.

Cream of Mushroom Soup

6 servings

2 cups chopped fresh mushrooms
½ teaspoon onion powder
⅛ teaspoon garlic powder
⅛ teaspoon white pepper

¼ teaspoon salt
2½ cups chicken broth
1 cup heavy cream

1. Combine mushrooms, seasonings, and broth in a 2-quart casserole.
2. Cook for 5 to 6 minutes, stirring once during cooking period.
3. Stir in cream.
4. Cook for 2 minutes, or until piping hot.

Superb Cream of Chicken

3 servings

1 can (10½ ounces) condensed cream
  of chicken soup, undiluted
1 soup can milk

1 pimiento, diced
¼ cup chopped ripe olives
½ teaspoon turmeric

1. Combine all ingredients in a 1-quart ovenproof bowl or measuring cup.
2. Cook for 5 to 5½ minutes, or until piping hot. Stir well before serving.

Cream Sudanese

6 servings

1 can (10½ ounces) condensed cream
  of tomato soup, undiluted
1 can (10½ ounces) condensed pea
  soup, undiluted

½ cup heavy cream
3 tablespoons sherry

1. Place both soups and 1½ soup cans of water in a 1½-quart ovenproof bowl. Stir to blend well.
2. Cook for 4 minutes.
3. Stir in cream and sherry.
4. Cook for 2 minutes, or until piping hot.

Egg Drop Soup

4 servings

2 cans (13¾ ounces) chicken broth
1 tablespoon cornstarch
1 can (4 ounces) water chestnuts, diced
2 scallions, chopped, including green
  tops

2 eggs, slightly beaten
Salt to taste

1. Put chicken broth in a 1½-quart casserole or mixing bowl.
2. Cook, covered, for 6 minutes.
3. Combine cornstarch with 2 tablespoons water. Stir in hot broth. Stir in water chestnuts and scallions.
4. Cook, covered, for 3 to 4 minutes, or until mixture is clear and piping hot.
5. Remove and quickly stir in beaten eggs. Taste and season with salt, if necessary.

Indienne Cream

6 servings

2 cans (10½ ounces each) condensed
  cream of celery soup, undiluted
2 soup cans milk

1 teaspoon curry powder
2 medium apples, peeled, cored, and
  diced

1. Place soup in a 2-quart ovenproof bowl. Stir in milk and curry powder, mixing well.
2. Cook for 4 to 5 minutes, or until piping hot.
3. Stir in apples. Cook for 1 minute.

Potato Parsley Soup

4 servings

3 cups peeled, cubed potatoes
¼ cup chopped onion
¼ teaspoon salt
1 can (14 ounces) chicken broth

1 small bunch parsley, chopped
2 tablespoons cornstarch
1½ to 2 cups milk

1. Combine potatoes, onion, salt, and broth in a 2-quart casserole. Add parsley.
2. Cook, covered, for 20 to 22 minutes, or until potatoes are tender.
3. Combine cornstarch with a small amount of cold milk. Stir into potato mixture. Add remaining milk.
4. Cook, uncovered, for about 5 minutes, or until mixture comes to a boil and is piping hot. Stir once or twice during cooking.

Cheese Soup

4 servings

2½ cups beef broth
½ cup chopped onions

½ teaspoon celery powder
1½ cups grated sharp Cheddar cheese

1. In a 2-quart bowl combine beef broth, onion, and celery powder.
2. Cook for 4½ minutes.
3. Stir in cheese, blending well.
4. Cook for 1 minute, or until cheese is melted.
5. Stir well before serving.

Cold Cucumber Soup

4 servings

2 cups chicken broth
3 large cucumbers
½ teaspoon salt

¼ teaspoon white pepper
1 tablespoon grated onion
1 cup light cream

1. Place chicken broth in a 2-quart ovenproof bowl.
2. Peel and dice 2 of the cucumbers and half of the third. Add to the chicken broth along with salt, pepper, and onion.
3. Cook for 6 to 7 minutes, or until cucumbers are tender.
4. Remove from oven and puree in a blender or force through a sieve. Cool.
5. Stir in cream and refrigerate.
6. Just before serving, float several slices of cucumber on top of each serving.

FOLLOWING PAGES: Left, *Cioppino*, page 26; right, *Quebec Green Pea Soup*, page 28.

Turkey Stock

2 quarts

1 turkey carcass from a 10-pound turkey (approximately)
2 stalks celery with leaves
1 small onion

1 teaspoon salt
½ teaspoon peppercorns
Pinch of mixed herbs

1. Strip all the meat from the turkey carcass. Break up body bones and place with leg and wing bones in a 3- or 4-quart casserole. Add remaining ingredients. Fill casserole a little over half full with water.
2. Cook, covered, for 1 hour to 1¼ hours.
3. Strain and use stock as desired.

Carrot Chowder

5 to 6 servings

4 slices bacon
1 can (1 pound) diced carrots
1 tablespoon grated onion

¼ cup finely diced celery
2 cups chicken broth

1. Cook bacon according to instructions on page 60. Crumble and reserve.
2. Place carrots, including liquid from can, in a 2-quart ovenproof bowl. Add remaining ingredients and stir well.
3. Cook for 5 to 6 minutes, or until piping hot.
4. Stir in crumbled bacon before serving.

Note: Three hard-cooked eggs peeled and chopped may be added to the chowder along with the bacon if desired.

Cioppino

8 servings

1 large onion, chopped
1 medium green pepper, seeded and chopped
½ cup thinly sliced celery
3 cloves garlic, minced
3 tablespoons olive oil
1 can (3 pounds 3 ounces) peeled Italian tomatoes with puree
1 can (8 ounces) tomato sauce
1 teaspoon basil
1 bay leaf

1 teaspoon salt
¼ teaspoon pepper
1 pound firm white fish
1 dozen mussels or littleneck clams in the shell
1½ cups dry white wine
½ pound whole shrimp, cleaned and deveined
½ pound scallops
Chopped parsley

1. Combine onion, pepper, celery, garlic, and olive oil in a 4-quart casserole.
2. Cook, uncovered, for about 7 minutes, or until onion is soft.
3. Mash tomatoes with a fork or potato masher so that whole tomatoes are broken up in small pieces. Add tomatoes to casserole. Add tomato sauce, basil, bay leaf, salt, and pepper.
4. Cook, covered, for about 20 minutes, to blend the flavors.
5. While sauce is cooking, cut white fish into serving pieces. Using a stiff

brush, thoroughly scrub the mussels, cutting off their beards, or soak clams in cold water to which a little cornmeal has been added and then scrub under cold running water to remove any residue of mud and sand. Stir wine into tomato mixture. Add white fish, shrimp, and scallops.

6. Cook, covered, for about 15 minutes.
7. Place mussels or clams in a layer on top of fish in casserole.
8. Cook, covered, for 12 to 15 minutes, or until shells are fully opened.
9. Discard any mussels or clams that are unopened.
10. Ladle soup into soup plates. Sprinkle with parsley and serve piping hot with French bread.

Clam Chowder
3 to 4 servings

2 slices bacon
1 can (7 ounces) minced clams, with liquid
1 large potato, peeled and cubed

¼ cup minced onion
1 can (13 ounces) evaporated milk
Salt and pepper to taste
1 tablespoon butter

1. Put bacon slices in a 2-quart casserole. Cover with a piece of paper towel.
2. Cook for about 4 minutes, or until bacon is crisp.
3. Remove paper towel and bacon, leaving drippings in casserole. Crumble bacon into bits and reserve. Add clams, clam liquid, potato, onion, and ½ cup water to casserole.
4. Cook, covered, for 13 minutes, or until potatoes are tender. Stir once or twice during cooking time.
5. Add milk, crumbled bacon, salt and pepper to taste, and butter.
6. Cook, covered, for about 5 minutes, or just until mixture comes to a boil.
7. Let stand 2 minutes. Serve with crumbled common crackers if desired.

Red Bean Soup
6 servings

8 slices bacon
2 tablespoons bacon drippings
1 large onion, diced
1 clove garlic, crushed

2 cans (27 ounces each) red kidney beans
½ teaspoon salt
1 can (8 ounces) tomato sauce

1. Cook bacon according to directions on page 60. Crumble and reserve.
2. Place bacon drippings in a 2-quart ovenproof casserole. Add onion and garlic and cook, covered, for 3 minutes.
3. Add ½ cup water and remaining ingredients, including liquid from the canned beans. Mix well.
4. Cook, covered, for 10 to 12 minutes, to blend flavors.
5. Puree soup in a blender, half at a time, and return to casserole. If soup is too thick, stir in enough water to make it the desired consistency.
6. Cook for 3 minutes, or until piping hot.
7. Stir in reserved bacon before serving.

Quebec Green Pea Soup

4 to 6 servings

1 can (2 ounces) mushroom stems
  and pieces
1 tablespoon butter or margarine

2 cans (11½ ounces) condensed
  green pea soup, undiluted
1 cup grated raw carrots

1. Drain mushrooms, pouring liquid into a measuring cup. Add enough water to make 2 cups of liquid.
2. Melt butter in a 1½- to 2-quart casserole for 30 seconds. Add drained mushrooms.
3. Cook, uncovered, for 4 to 5 minutes, or just until heated.
4. Add soup and mushroom-water mixture. Stir until well blended. Stir in grated carrots.
5. Cook, covered, for 9 to 10 minutes, or just until carrots are crisply tender.
6. Taste and season if necessary. Serve with croutons or crackers.

Spring Pea Soup

4 servings

1 package (10 ounces) frozen peas
3 cups chicken broth
6 scallions, sliced

¼ teaspoon white pepper
½ cup heavy cream

1. Place peas in a 1½-quart ovenproof casserole. Add chicken broth, scallions, and pepper.
2. Cook, covered, for 10 to 11 minutes, stirring once.
3. Stir in cream, taste, and add salt if necessary.
4. Cook for 1 minute.

Note: If desired, after Step 2, puree soup in a blender or force through a sieve. Proceed with Step 3.

Chili Chowder

6 servings

¾ pound ground beef
1 medium onion, chopped
1 clove garlic, chopped
2 tablespoons chopped green pepper
1 can (1 pound) peeled plum tomatoes

2 cups tomato juice
1 teaspoon salt
⅛ teaspoon sugar
2 teaspoons chili powder, or to taste

1. Place beef, onion, garlic, and green pepper in a 2-quart ovenproof casserole.
2. Cook, covered, for 5 to 6 minutes.
3. Remove casserole and stir to break up beef.
4. Add tomatoes, including liquid from can, stirring to break up tomatoes.
5. Add remaining ingredients and mix well.
6. Cook, covered, for 6 to 7 minutes, or until piping hot.

Meats

Roasts, chops, hamburgers, and small cuts of tender meat cook beautifully in the microwave oven. Pot roasts and tough cuts that require long, slow cooking will do better in the conventional range or oven.

A large piece of meat, especially if the shape is uneven, should be turned and rotated for uniform roasting. If overdone spots appear, cover with small pieces of aluminum foil to slow or halt the cooking in these places. Be sure to remove the roast before it reaches "done" temperature, as it continues to cook after being removed from the microwave oven. Let it stand until the desired degree of doneness is reached. If the meat does not reach the temperature desired, it is a simple matter to return it to the microwave oven for just a few minutes longer.

Rolled Ribs of Beef
8 to 10 servings

4- to 5-pound rolled rib of beef roast   **Seasoned salt (optional)**
1 clove garlic, cut in slivers

1. Place an inverted saucer in the bottom of a baking dish. Poke holes in meat with a sharp knife and insert a thin sliver of garlic in each slit. Sprinkle roast with seasoned salt. Place roast fat side down on saucer.
2. Cook, uncovered, for about 3½ minutes per pound for rare, 4½ minutes for medium.
3. Turn fat side up. Cover with waxed paper to prevent fat from splattering oven walls. Cook, covered, about 3½ minutes per pound for rare, 4½ minutes for medium.
4. Remove roast, insert a thermometer halfway into meat, not fat, to obtain the desired reading.
5. If reading is correct, cover roast tightly with foil and let stand about 15 minutes to bring meat up to desired temperature.

Standing Ribs of Beef
6 to 8 servings

1 rib roast of beef, with at least 2 bones   **Salt to taste**
1 clove garlic, slivered

1. Place an inverted saucer in the bottom of an oblong baking dish. Make slits in beef with a sharp knife and insert a thin sliver of garlic in each slit. Sprinkle roast with salt. Place roast, fat side down, on saucer in baking dish. Cover bones with a small piece of aluminum foil.
2. Cook, uncovered, for about 3½ minutes per pound for rare, 4½ minutes for medium.
3. Remove pieces of foil. Turn ribs fat side up. Cover roast with a piece of waxed paper to prevent fat from splattering oven walls. Cook, covered, for about 3½ minutes per pound for rare, 4½ minutes for medium.
4. Remove roast, insert a thermometer into heavy part of meat, making sure that it does not touch the bone.
5. If reading is correct, cover roast tightly with aluminum foil and let stand at least 15 minutes to bring meat up to desired temperature and to make it easier to carve. If desired temperature has not been reached, remove thermometer and return meat to the oven for 1 to 2 minutes.

Roasting Time, Temperature for Rolled Roast, Ribs of Beef

Note: It is not recommended to roast meat until well done in microwave oven. If meat has been standing at room temperature for 1 hour or more before roasting, reduce cooking time by ½ minute for each pound of meat.

	Minutes per pound for Rare	Minutes per pound for Medium
	6 to 7	8 to 9
Internal Temperature (measured on meat thermometer)	120°; will rise to 140° on standing	140°; will rise to 160° on standing

To thaw an eye round roast of beef:

1 frozen eye round roast of beef, 3½ to 4 pounds

1. Place roast in a casserole with a cover.
2. Heat for 5 minutes, rotating casserole midway in cooking period. Let stand for 10 minutes.
3. Heat for 5 minutes, rotating casserole midway in cooking period. Let stand for 10 minutes.
4. Heat for 4 minutes, rotating casserole midway in cooking period. Let stand for 10 minutes.
5. Heat for 4 minutes, rotating casserole midway in cooking period. Let stand for 10 minutes.
6. Cook as soon as possible, since in the thawing process parts of the meat have begun to cook.

Eye Round Roast of Beef   8 servings

3½- to 4-pound eye round of beef   Salt and pepper

1. Place 1 or 2 saucers upside down in an oblong roasting pan. Place roast fat side down on top of saucers.
2. Cook, covered with a piece of waxed paper, for 10 minutes.
3. Turn piece of meat over. Drain off accumulated fat and drippings. Replace waxed paper covering.
4. Cook for 18 to 20 minutes, or until meat reaches an internal temperature of 125°.
5. Remove waxed paper. Cover with foil and let stand 15 to 20 minutes, or until meat reaches a temperature of 145° for medium rare.
6. Season with salt and pepper to taste, slice, and serve.

Roasting Time for Eye Round of Beef

Minutes per pound for rare	Minutes per pound for medium
about 6	7 to 7½

To thaw sirloin steak:

1 frozen 3-pound sirloin steak, 1½ inches thick

1. Place steak in a 3-quart flat dish. Cover with plastic wrap.
2. Heat for 4 minutes. Let stand 10 minutes.
3. Turn steak over and cover with plastic wrap.
4. Heat for 4 minutes. Let stand 10 minutes.
5. Turn steak over. Cover. Heat for another 4 minutes. Let stand 10 more minutes, or until steak is thawed and ready for broiling.

31

FOLLOWING PAGES: Left, *Standing Ribs of Beef, page 30;* right, *Beef Tacos, page 47.*

Beef Goulash

4 servings

2 pounds stew beef, cut in 1-inch
cubes
3 to 4 large tomatoes
1 onion, coarsely chopped

1 teaspoon salt
½ teaspoon freshly ground pepper
1 cup sour cream (optional)

1. Place beef in a 2- to 3-quart casserole.
2. Peel tomatoes; remove cores. Cut tomatoes in chunks. Place in casserole
   with beef, onion, salt, and pepper. Toss mixture lightly.
3. Cook, covered, for at least 1 hour, or until beef is tender. Stir occasionally during cooking period.
4. If desired, stir sour cream into mixture and let stand, covered, 5 minutes.

Note: This is excellent served with cooked egg noodles.

Quick Beef Casserole

4 servings

1 package (10 ounces) frozen
French-style green beans
1 pound stew beef, cut in cubes
1 large onion, chopped

1 can (10½ ounces) condensed tomato
soup, undiluted
2 cups cooked egg noodles
Salt and pepper

1. Place green beans in a 1-quart casserole, icy side up.
2. Cook, covered, for 8 to 10 minutes. Reserve.
3. Combine beef cubes and onion in a 2- to 3-quart casserole.
4. Cook, covered with waxed paper, for 8 to 10 minutes, stirring halfway
   through cooking time.
5. Add tomato soup, ½ cup water, noodles, and green beans to beef cubes.
   Stir lightly and season with salt and pepper to taste.
6. Cook, covered, for 8 to 9 minutes.
7. Stir and let stand, covered, 3 to 4 minutes before serving.

Short Ribs of Beef

4 servings

2 pounds meaty short ribs of beef
1 clove garlic, minced
½ teaspoon salt

½ cup-dry red wine
1 tablespoon liquid gravy seasoning
Chopped parsley

1. Arrange short ribs in a 2- or 3-quart casserole. Sprinkle with garlic and
   salt. Combine wine and liquid gravy seasoning. Pour over short ribs.
2. Cook, covered, for about 30 minutes, or until meat is tender, stirring once
   or twice during cooking period.
3. Remove and let stand 5 minutes.

Tomato Swiss Steak

4 servings

¼ cup all-purpose flour
1 teaspoon salt
¼ teaspoon pepper
1½ to 2 pounds round steak

1 large onion, chopped
1 can (10½ ounces) condensed tomato
  soup, undiluted

1. Combine flour, salt, and pepper. Place steak on a board and pound half of the flour mixture into each side of steak with the back of a heavy knife. Cut meat in 4 pieces and place in an 8-inch baking dish. Sprinkle any remaining flour over top of meat. Spread onion over meat. Combine tomato soup with ½ cup water. Pour over steak.
2. Cook, covered, for about 50 minutes, or until meat is tender. Stir meat and sauce several times during cooking period and add a little additional water if necessary.

Onion Steak

4 servings

¼ cup all-purpose flour
1 teaspoon salt
¼ teaspoon pepper

1½ to 2 pounds round steak
½ package (1⅓ ounces) onion soup
  mix

1. Combine flour, salt, and pepper. Place steak on a board and pound half of the flour mixture into each side of steak with the back of a heavy knife. Cut meat in 4 pieces and place in an 8-inch baking dish. Sprinkle any remaining flour over top of meat. Combine onion soup mix with 1 cup water. Pour over top of meat.
2. Cook, covered, for about 50 minutes, or until meat is tender. Stir and rearrange meat in sauce several times during cooking period.

Beef Stew

4 to 6 servings

2 pounds stew meat, cut in 1-inch
  cubes
½ teaspoon salt
1 package (1½ ounces) brown gravy
  mix with mushrooms

3 stalks celery, cut in pieces
3 medium carrots, cut in small chunks
2 medium potatoes, peeled and cut
  in eighths

1. Put beef cubes in a 2- to 3-quart casserole. Sprinkle with salt. Combine gravy mix with 1 cup water and stir well. Pour over meat.
2. Cook, covered, for about 30 minutes, or until meat is almost tender.
3. Add celery, carrots, and potatoes and stir lightly so that vegetables are covered with gravy. Add more water for a thinner gravy and a little additional salt for the vegetables, if desired.
4. Cook, covered, for about 20 minutes, or until vegetables and meat are tender.
5. Remove and let stand 5 minutes.

FOLLOWING PAGES: Left, *Beef Stew, page 35;* right, *Shish Kabob, page 38.*

Shish Kabob

6 to 8 servings

½ cup wine vinegar
½ cup cooking oil
1 teaspoon onion salt
1 clove garlic, split in half
¼ cup soy sauce
2 teaspoons Italian seasoning
2 pounds boneless sirloin or top round steak

½ pound small fresh mushrooms
1 dozen tomato wedges or cherry tomatoes
1 green pepper, seeded and cut in 1-inch squares

1. Combine vinegar, oil, onion salt, garlic, soy sauce, Italian seasoning, and ½ cup water in a large mixing bowl. Cut steak in 1-inch cubes. Add to marinade and let stand at room temperature 5 to 6 hours.
2. Place meat cubes and desired vegetables alternately on long wooden skewers.
3. Place 2 or 3 skewers on a dinner plate.
4. Cook, uncovered, for 7 to 8 minutes, for medium rare. Cook slightly longer for well-done meat.

Note: The marinade turns the meat brown while standing, for attractive color in the finished kabobs.

Beef and Peppers

4 servings

2 tablespoons cooking oil
1 pound top round or sirloin steak, cut into thin strips
1 medium onion, finely chopped
1 clove garlic, minced
1 teaspoon salt

⅛ teaspoon pepper
1 can (1 pound) tomatoes, broken up
2 large green peppers, seeded and cut in strips
2 tablespoons soy sauce

1. Put oil in a 2- or 3-quart casserole or baking dish. Add beef strips and toss lightly so that meat is coated with oil. Add onion, garlic, salt, and pepper.
2. Cook, covered, for 9 to 10 minutes, stirring once or twice during cooking period.
3. Add tomatoes. Cook, covered, for 6 minutes, stirring once during cooking period.
4. Add green pepper strips and soy sauce and toss thoroughly.
5. Cook, covered, for 6 to 7 minutes, or just until green pepper is tender but still crisp.
6. Serve with hot cooked rice or chow mein noodles.

To thaw frozen ground beef:

1 pound ground beef, frozen in a flat square (about 1 inch high)

1. Place in an 8-inch square baking dish.
2. Heat for 2 minutes. Let stand 1 minute.
3. Heat again for 2 minutes. Let stand 1 minute.
4. With fork break off outside pieces that have thawed, leaving frozen center. Place thawed pieces in a mixing bowl and set aside so that they will not cook.
5. Heat frozen center of meat for 1 minute. Let stand 1 minute.
6. Break off more of the thawed meat and set aside.
7. Heat frozen part for 1 minute. Let stand 1 minute.
8. The meat should now be completely thawed and ready to use in ground beef dishes, such as meatballs and meat loaf. Once meat is defrosted it should be used immediately.

2 pounds ground beef, in a flat square

1. Place in an 8-inch square baking dish.
2. Heat for 2 minutes. Let stand 1 minute.
3. Heat again for 2 minutes. Let stand 1 minute.
4. With fork break off outside pieces that have thawed, leaving frozen center. Place thawed pieces in a mixing bowl and set aside so that they will not cook.
5. Heat frozen center of meat for 2 minutes. Let stand 1 minute.
6. Break off more of the thawed meat and set aside.
7. Heat frozen part for 1 minute. Let stand 1 minute.
8. If meat is not completely thawed at this point, heat for 2 minutes.
9. Once completely thawed, meat should be used immediately.

Nutty Meatballs   4 servings

1 pound lean ground beef	2 tablespoons chopped parsley
1 egg, lightly beaten	½ teaspoon salt
¼ cup milk	Freshly ground pepper to taste
½ cup soft bread crumbs	1 can (10½ ounces) condensed tomato
½ cup chopped pecans	soup, undiluted

1. Combine ground beef with egg, milk, bread crumbs, pecans, parsley, salt, and pepper. Blend well. Shape mixture into 24 meatballs. Arrange in an oblong baking dish.
2. Cook, covered, for 7 minutes.
3. Turn meatballs over. Cook again for 3 minutes.
4. Drain off fat and liquid. Add tomato soup. Blend lightly. Cook, covered, for 5 minutes, or until piping hot, stirring once or twice during cooking period.
5. Let stand 5 minutes before serving.
6. Serve over hot mashed potatoes.

Onion Meatballs

1½ pounds lean ground beef
½ cup milk
1 package (1¼ ounces) onion soup
mix

3 tablespoons all-purpose flour
2 tablespoons chopped parsley
½ cup dairy sour cream

1. In a large bowl combine beef with milk and 2 tablespoons of the onion soup mix. Mix thoroughly. Shape into 24 meatballs. Place in a 3-quart oblong baking dish.
2. Cook, covered, for 7 minutes.
3. Turn meatballs over. Cook, covered, for 3 minutes.
4. Remove meatballs. Stir flour into drippings in dish. Stir in 1½ cups water, parsley, and remaining soup mix.
5. Cook, uncovered, for about 5 minutes, or until mixture comes to a boil.
6. Add meatballs. Cook, covered, for 8 minutes, stirring occasionally during cooking period.
7. Gradually blend in sour cream. Cover and let stand 5 minutes before serving.
8. Serve over rice or noodles.

Meatballs Stroganoff

5 to 6 servings

¾ cup milk
3 slices bread, cubed
1 pound ground beef
1 egg, lightly beaten
3 tablespoons grated onion
3 tablespoons dried parsley flakes
1 teaspoon salt

Freshly ground pepper to taste
3 tablespoons flour
1½ cups beef broth or bouillon
1 tablespoon tomato paste
¼ teaspoon paprika
1½ cups dairy sour cream

1. Pour milk into a mixing bowl. Cook in oven for 1¾ minutes, or just long enough to warm milk.
2. Add bread cubes and mix until all the milk is absorbed by the bread.
3. Add beef, egg, onion, parsley, salt, and pepper. Blend well. Form mixture into balls about 1½ inches in diameter. Arrange meatballs in a 7¼- by 11¾-inch oblong baking dish.
4. Cook, covered, for 7 minutes.
5. Turn meatballs over and cook again for 3 minutes. Drain off fat and liquid.
6. Stir together flour and beef broth to make a smooth mixture. Stir in tomato paste and paprika. Pour mixture over top of meatballs.
7. Cook, covered, for 8 minutes, stirring often after 5 minutes of cooking time.
8. Top with sour cream and stir lightly. Cover and let stand about 5 minutes before serving.
9. Serve with cooked rice or hot buttered noodles.

41

OPPOSITE: *Beef and Peppers, page 38.*

Herbed Meat Loaf
6 servings

2 eggs, lightly beaten
¼ cup bread crumbs
1 tablespoon chopped parsley
¼ cup chopped chives or onion
1 tablespoon dried basil
¼ cup chopped green pepper

1½ teaspoons salt
½ teaspoon pepper
1 pound ground beef
½ pound ground veal
½ pound lean ground pork

1. Combine all ingredients except meat, and mix well. Add ground meat and blend with hands, being careful not to mix more than necessary.
2. Shape into a round and place in an 8-inch pie plate. Make a depression in center of loaf.
3. Cook, uncovered, for 25 minutes, or until center of loaf is cooked.
4. Remove. Cover meat and let stand 10 minutes before serving.
5. Serve with mushroom gravy or tomato sauce, if desired.

Note: Use caution when slicing, since meat juices tend to squirt when meat is sliced.

Our Favorite Meat Loaf
6 servings

1 can (8 ounces) tomato sauce
¼ cup brown sugar
¼ cup vinegar
1 teaspoon prepared mustard
1 egg, lightly beaten

1 medium onion, minced
¼ cup cracker crumbs
2 pounds ground beef
1½ teaspoons salt
¼ teaspoon pepper

1. Combine tomato sauce, brown sugar, vinegar, and mustard in a small bowl. Set aside.
2. Combine egg, onion, cracker crumbs, ground beef, salt, and pepper in a mixing bowl. Add ½ cup of the tomato mixture and blend thoroughly. Shape into an oval loaf and place in an oblong baking dish. Make a depression in top of loaf. Pour remaining tomato sauce over top of meat.
3. Cook, uncovered, for 25 to 30 minutes, or until center of loaf is cooked.
4. Cover meat and let stand about 10 minutes before serving.

Vegetable Meat Loaf
6 servings

1 can (10½ ounces) condensed
   vegetable soup, undiluted
2 pounds lean ground beef
½ cup fine dry bread crumbs
½ cup chopped onions
2 tablespoons chopped parsley

1 tablespoon Worcestershire sauce
1 egg, lightly beaten
1 teaspoon salt
Freshly ground pepper to taste
4 tomato slices
½ cup grated process American cheese

1. Combine soup, beef, bread crumbs, onion, parsley, Worcestershire, egg, salt, and pepper. Mix thoroughly. Shape into an oval loaf and place in an oblong baking dish. Make a slight depression in the top of the loaf.

2. Cook, covered with a piece of waxed paper, for 25 to 30 minutes, or until center of loaf is cooked.
3. Place tomato slices and cheese on top of loaf. Cook, uncovered, for about 4 minutes.
4. Let stand 5 minutes before serving.

Vintage Meat Loaf   6 servings

2 tablespoons dry red wine
2 tablespoons milk
1 cup soft bread crumbs
2 pounds lean ground beef
1 egg, lightly beaten

2 tablespoons minced onion
¾ teaspoon salt
Freshly ground pepper to taste
½ teaspoon dry mustard
½ teaspoon mixed herbs

1. Put red wine and milk in a mixing bowl with bread crumbs. Let stand a few minutes for bread to absorb the liquid. Add beef, egg, onion, salt, pepper, mustard, and herbs. Mix lightly until completely blended. Pack mixture in a 8- by 4- by 3-inch loaf dish.
2. Cover loaf with a piece of waxed paper. Cook, covered, for 12 minutes, rotating dish midway in cooking period, or until meat is done in center.
3. Remove and let stand, covered, 5 minutes before serving.

Gus's Cabbage Rolls   6 to 8 servings

1 head cabbage, about 1½ pounds
1 pound ground beef
½ pound ground pork
¾ cup cooked rice
1 egg, lightly beaten
1 teaspoon thyme

1 tablespoon chopped parsley
1 clove garlic, minced
1 tablespoon salt
¼ teaspoon pepper
¼ cup butter or margarine

1. Remove core from cabbage. Remove any blemished leaves. Put cabbage in a 3-quart casserole. Add boiling water to cover about one-quarter of the bottom of the cabbage.
2. Cook, covered, for 13 to 14 minutes.
3. Cool cabbage slightly and remove 6 to 8 of the large outside leaves. Remove the tough center core from each leaf.
4. Combine ground beef, pork, rice, egg, thyme, parsley, garlic, salt, and pepper. Toss together lightly. Divide mixture among cabbage leaves. Wrap leaves tightly around mixture.
5. Line bottom of a 3-quart casserole with some of the leftover cabbage leaves. Place rolled cabbage packets on top of loose leaves. Cover with remaining pieces of cabbage.
6. Top with butter. Add about 1½ cups boiling water.
7. Cook, covered, for about 1 hour, or until meat is cooked and rolls are fork-tender.
8. Remove and let stand, covered, 10 minutes.
9. Discard the top loose cabbage leaves before serving.

43

FOLLOWING PAGES: Left, *Chili con Carne*, page 46; right, *Curried Lamb*, page 51.

Broccoli and Beef

2 servings

1 large or 2 medium stalks broccoli
2 tablespoons cooking oil
½ cup coarsely chopped onions
1 clove garlic, minced

½ pound ground beef
½ cup thinly sliced celery
2 teaspoons soy sauce
1 tablespoon dry sherry

1. Cut off flowerets from top of broccoli and cut large flowers in halves or quarters. Peel broccoli stalks and cut in diagonal slices about ½ inch thick. Set aside.
2. In a 1½-quart casserole place oil, onion, and garlic. Add beef, broken into pieces.
3. Cook, covered, for 6 minutes.
4. Remove casserole and break up pieces of beef with a fork. Add celery, soy sauce, sherry, and broccoli. Stir.
5. Cook, covered, for 6 minutes, or just until broccoli is crisply tender.
6. Serve over hot cooked rice with additional soy sauce.

Hamburger Hash Burgundy

4 servings

1 pound ground beef
½ cup chopped onions
2 tablespoons all-purpose flour
1 can (10½ ounces) condensed beef consomme, undiluted

½ cup dry red wine
2 cups diced raw potatoes
½ cup diced celery
Salt and pepper to taste

1. Crumble ground beef into a 2-quart casserole. Stir in onion.
2. Cook, uncovered, for 4 minutes.
3. Stir with a fork to break up meat. Cook for 3 to 4 minutes, or until meat loses its red color.
4. Sprinkle flour on meat. Stir in well. Add consomme and wine.
5. Cook, covered, for about 5 minutes, or until liquid becomes warm.
6. Add potatoes and celery, and salt and pepper to taste.
7. Cook, covered, for 40 to 45 minutes, or until potatoes are tender.
8. Let stand 5 minutes before serving.

Chili con Carne

4 servings

1 pound ground beef
½ cup chopped onions
1 clove garlic, minced
2 to 3 teaspoons chili powder

1 teaspoon salt
1 can (16 ounces) tomato sauce
1 can (1 pound) kidney beans

1. Crumble ground beef in a 2-quart casserole. Add onion and garlic.
2. Cook, uncovered, for 7 to 8 minutes, or until meat loses its red color.
3. Add remaining ingredients. Cook, covered, for 12 to 15 minutes, or until piping hot. Stir occasionally during cooking period.

Variation: Omit chili powder and salt and use half a package (1¾ ounces) chili mix.

Limas and Beef Casserole

4 to 6 servings

1 pound lean ground beef
1 clove garlic, crushed
1 medium onion, chopped
1 small green pepper, seeded and
  chopped
¼ teaspoon chili powder

½ teaspoon dry mustard
2 teaspoons Worcestershire sauce
½ teaspoon salt
2 cans (1 pound each) lima beans
1 can (8 ounces) tomato sauce

1. Combine beef, garlic, onion, and green pepper in a 2- or 3-quart casserole.
2. Cook, uncovered, for 7 to 8 minutes, or until beef loses its pink color. Stir once or twice during cooking period to break up meat.
3. Add remaining ingredients. Toss lightly.
4. Cook, covered, for about 12 minutes, stirring once during cooking period.
5. Let stand, covered, 3 to 4 minutes before serving.

Beef Tacos

10 to 12 servings

1 pound ground beef
½ cup chopped onions
1 can (8 ounces) tomato sauce
¼ teaspoon chili powder
¼ teaspoon salt
¼ teaspoon garlic salt

10 to 12 fully cooked taco shells
Grated Cheddar cheese
Shredded lettuce
Chopped fresh tomato
Finely diced avocado

1. Crumble beef into a 1-quart casserole. Add onion.
2. Cook for about 5 minutes, or until meat loses its pink color, stirring once.
3. Add tomato sauce, chili powder, salt, and garlic salt.
4. Cover casserole with a paper towel. Cook for 7 to 8 minutes, or until sauce is blended and thickened.
5. Spoon filling into taco shells. Place tacos in a straight-sided glass dish so they will stand upright.
6. Cook, covered with waxed paper, for 3 to 4 minutes, or until tacos are piping hot.
7. Serve with cheese, lettuce, tomato, and avocado in side dishes to sprinkle as desired over top of hot filling.

FOLLOWING PAGES: Left, *Veal Parmigiana, page 54;* right, *Barbecued Spareribs, page 58.*

Burger Stroganoff

4 to 6 servings

1 pound ground beef
½ cup minced onions
1 clove garlic, minced
1 pound fresh mushrooms, sliced
2 teaspoons salt
¼ teaspoon pepper
2 tablespoons all-purpose flour
1 cup dairy sour cream
Minced parsley

1. Crumble beef into a 1½-quart casserole. Add onion and garlic.
2. Cook, uncovered, for 4 to 5 minutes.
3. Stir with a fork to break up meat. Add mushrooms.
4. Cook, covered, for 4 to 5 minutes.
5. Sprinkle salt, pepper, and flour over top of meat. Stir lightly.
6. Cook, covered, for 3 minutes, stirring at the end of 1 minute.
7. Stir in sour cream. Cover and let stand 2 minutes. If mixture is not warm enough, cook, covered, for 1 to 2 minutes, or until heated. *Do not let mixture boil.*
8. Serve over hot cooked noodles or mashed potatoes.

Leg of Lamb

8 servings

4- to 4½-pound leg of lamb, bone in
1 large clove garlic, cut in thin slices
Salt and pepper to taste

1. Cut small slits in both sides of leg of lamb. Insert thin slices of garlic in slits.
2. Place a saucer upside down in an oblong baking dish. Place leg of lamb fat side up on saucer.
3. Cook, uncovered, for about 24 minutes.
4. Turn leg of lamb over so that fat side is down. Cook, uncovered, for about 24 minutes. Sprinkle lightly with salt and pepper.
5. Remove from oven and insert thermometer in meat, being sure to not touch the bone. Thermometer should register 160°.
6. Leave thermometer in meat and cover tightly with aluminum foil; let stand about 20 minutes or until thermometer registers 180°.

Note: The times given are for well-done lamb. For pink lamb, decrease cooking time.

Cooking Time for Leg of Lamb

Rare	Medium
10 to 11 minutes per pound	12 minutes per pound

Bill's Lamb Chops

4 servings

4 shoulder lamb chops
½ cup coarsely chopped onion
1 clove garlic, minced

½ cup catsup
2 tablespoons Worcestershire sauce
1 tablespoon prepared mustard

1. In a baking dish arrange lamb chops in one layer. Sprinkle with onion and garlic. Cook, uncovered, for 5 to 7 minutes.
2. Combine remaining ingredients and spread over lamb chops. Cook, covered, for 20 to 22 minutes, or until lamb chops are tender.

Lamb Stew

4 servings

1 pound boneless lamb, cut in 1-inch cubes
1 package (⅝ ounce) brown gravy mix
2 tablespoons all-purpose flour
1 teaspoon salt
⅛ teaspoon pepper

1 clove garlic, minced
½ teaspoon Worcestershire sauce
¼ cup red wine
3 medium carrots, peeled and cut in chunks
2 stalks celery, cut in pieces
2 potatoes, peeled and cut in cubes

1. In a 2- or 3-quart casserole combine lamb and gravy mix.
2. Cook, uncovered, for 7 to 10 minutes, stirring occasionally.
3. Add remaining ingredients, with 1 cup of water. Stir well.
4. Cook, covered, for 35 minutes, or until meat and vegetables are tender. Stir occasionally during cooking time.
5. Let stand 3 to 4 minutes before serving.

Curried Lamb

4 servings

1 pound boneless lamb, cut in 1-inch cubes
2 tablespoons all-purpose flour
1 clove garlic, minced
1 large onion, sliced
¼ cup butter or margarine

1½ tablespoons curry powder
2 apples, peeled, cored, and chopped in coarse pieces
2 tablespoons seedless raisins
1½ teaspoons salt

1. Toss lamb cubes lightly with flour. Set aside.
2. Place garlic, onion, and butter in a 2-quart casserole. Cook, uncovered, for 5 minutes.
3. Add lamb and curry powder and toss lightly.
4. Cook, uncovered, for 15 minutes, stirring occasionally.
5. Add apples, raisins, and salt. Stir in ½ cup water.
6. Cook, covered, for 20 to 23 minutes, or until meat is tender. Stir occasionally during cooking time.
7. Let stand 3 minutes.
8. Serve with hot cooked rice and accompaniments such as flaked coconut, chopped peanuts or walnuts, and chutney.

51

FOLLOWING PAGES: Left, *Sweet and Sour Pork, page 58;* right, *Stuffed Pork Chops, page 57.*

Veal Elegante

3 to 4 servings

1 pound boneless veal, cut in cubes
½ cup minced onions
1 fresh tomato, peeled and cubed
½ cup dry white wine
Salt and pepper to taste

1. Combine veal, onion, tomatoes, wine, and salt and pepper to taste in a 1½-quart casserole.
2. Cook, covered, for 35 to 40 minutes, or until veal is tender. Stir several times during cooking period; if sauce becomes dry, add a little more white wine or water.
3. Let stand 3 to 4 minutes. Serve over hot cooked rice or cooked buttered noodles.

Veal Parmigiana

4 servings

1 egg, lightly beaten
¼ teaspoon salt
3 tablespoons cracker crumbs
⅓ cup grated Parmesan cheese
1 pound veal cutlets
2 tablespoons cooking oil
¼ cup dry vermouth
1 medium onion, chopped
1 cup (4 ounces) sliced or shredded mozzarella cheese
1 can (8 ounces) tomato sauce
Grind of fresh pepper
⅛ teaspoon oregano

1. Beat egg with salt in a shallow dish. Combine cracker crumbs and Parmesan cheese on a piece of waxed paper. Cut veal into 4 serving pieces. Place each piece between two pieces of waxed paper and pound to about ¼ inch thick with the side of a cleaver.
2. Dip veal in egg and then in cracker crumbs. Heat oil in a skillet on top of the range. Cook veal in hot oil until golden brown on both sides.
3. Place veal in a 10- by 6-inch baking dish. Add vermouth to skillet and heat about 1 minute, scraping up browned bits from bottom of skillet. Pour over veal cutlets.
4. Sprinkle onion over meat. Top with mozzarella cheese. Spoon tomato sauce over top, and season with pepper and oregano.
5. Cook, covered, for 12 minutes, or until sauce is bubbly and cheese is melted.

Cordon Bleu Veal

2 servings

½ pound veal round steak or cutlets, cut ½-inch thick
1 slice Swiss cheese
2 thin slices boiled ham
1½ tablespoons all-purpose flour
1 egg
¼ cup dry bread crumbs
1½ tablespoons butter or margarine
1 tablespoon chopped parsley
1 tablespoon dry white wine

1. Cut veal into 4 pieces. Place each piece of veal between 2 pieces of waxed paper and pound with the side of a cleaver or a mallet until it is ⅛ inch thick.
2. Cut cheese in 2 pieces. Fold each piece of cheese in half. Place on a slice

of ham. Roll ham around cheese three times so that finished roll of ham is smaller than the pieces of veal. Place ham on one slice of veal and top with a second slice. Press edges of veal together to seal.
3. Put flour on a piece of waxed paper. Beat egg lightly with 1 tablespoon water. Put bread crumbs on a piece of waxed paper. Dip veal in flour, then in beaten egg, and finally coat well with bread crumbs.
4. Put butter and parsley in an 8-inch baking dish.
5. Cook in oven for 1½ minutes, or just long enough to heat butter well.
6. Add veal to very hot butter.
7. Cook, uncovered, for 3 minutes. Turn veal slices over.
8. Cook for 3 minutes, or just until lightly browned and crusty.
9. Pour wine over veal and tilt pan to swish wine around. Serve immediately.

Loin of Pork

6 to 8 servings

1 4-pound loin of pork

1. Place an inverted saucer in the bottom of an oblong baking dish that is large enough so that pork loin does not hang over the sides. Place pork fat side down on baking dish. Cover protruding bones with pieces of foil.
2. Cook for 28 minutes.
3. Remove foil and turn roast fat side up. Cook, covered loosely with waxed paper, for 28 minutes, or until meat thermometer registers 160°.
4. Let stand, covered with foil, until meat registers cooking time for pork on meat thermometer.

Note: Loin of pork should be cooked about 14½ minutes per pound. When meat is being cooked, fat side up (Step 3), you may season it very lightly with salt and pepper or brush it very lightly with a barbecue sauce to give it a brown color when served.

Orange Ginger Pork Chops

6 servings

6 lean pork chops	**1 teaspoon ground ginger**
¼ cup orange juice	**1 large orange, peeled and sliced**
½ teaspoon salt	**Dairy sour cream**

1. Trim fat from pork chops. Place in an oblong baking dish. Pour orange juice over chops.
2. Cook, covered, for 15 minutes.
3. Remove from oven. Turn chops over. Sprinkle with salt and ginger. Place an orange slice on top of each chop.
4. Cook, covered, for 17 minutes, or until chops are tender.
5. Remove from oven. Top each chop with a dollop of sour cream. Cover and let stand 5 minutes before serving.

Pork Chops with Apricots

4 servings

4 center-cut pork chops, about 1½ pounds

2 tablespoons brown sugar

½ teaspoon oregano

Salt and pepper to taste

1 can (8¾ ounces) apricot halves

1. Trim all fat from pork chops. Place chops in an 8-inch square baking dish. Sprinkle brown sugar, oregano, salt, and pepper on each chop. Pour half of the liquid from the apricots over chops.
2. Cook, covered, for 15 minutes; turn chops over and spoon liquid over chops. Cook 10 minutes more.
3. Remove from oven. Turn chops over. Spoon some of liquid from bottom of dish over chops. Cover chops with apricots.
4. Cook, covered, for 7 minutes, or until pork is tender.
5. Let stand 5 minutes before serving.

Stuffed Pork Chops

4 servings

1 cup coarse dry bread crumbs

¾ cup chopped apples

3 tablespoons chopped raisins

½ teaspoon salt

2 tablespoons sugar

2 tablespoons finely minced onion

Freshly ground pepper to taste

Pinch of sage

2 tablespoons melted butter or margarine

8 thin rib or loin pork chops

½ package (⅝ ounce) brown gravy mix

1. Combine bread crumbs, apples, raisins, salt, sugar, onion, pepper, sage, and melted butter. Toss together lightly. Moisten slightly with hot water if stuffing is dry.
2. Trim all fat from pork chops. Place 4 chops in bottom of an 8-inch square baking dish. Divide stuffing into 4 portions and place one portion on top of each chop. Cover chops with 4 remaining chops, pressing together lightly.
3. Sprinkle brown gravy mix over top of chops. (To make an even layer, sift mixture through a small strainer.)
4. Cook, uncovered, for 30 to 33 minutes, or until pork is tender.

Tomatoed Pork Chops

4 servings

4 center-cut pork chops

1 large onion, sliced

1 can (15 ounces) tomato sauce

Dash of hot-pepper sauce

¼ teaspoon marjoram

1. Trim all fat from chops. Place chops in an 8-inch square baking dish. Cover with sliced onion. Combine tomato sauce, hot-pepper sauce, and marjoram. Pour mixture over chops.
2. Cook, covered, for 15 minutes.
3. Remove from oven. Turn chops over. Spoon some of the sauce in bottom of dish over chops.
4. Cook, covered, for 17 minutes.
5. Allow to stand 5 minutes before serving.

57

OPPOSITE: *Baked Ham Steak, page 59.*

Sweet and Sour Pork

6 servings

1½ pounds lean pork shoulder, cut in
    ½-inch cubes
1 small onion, sliced
1 teaspoon salt
1 can (8 ounces) pineapple slices

1 package (2 ounces) sweet and sour
    mix
2 green peppers, seeded and cut in
    squares

1. Put pork cubes, onion, and salt in a 2- to 3-quart baking dish or casserole.
2. Cook, covered, for 18 to 19 minutes. Stir once or twice.
3. Drain off pork fat.
4. Drain pineapple slices, reserving juice. Add enough water to pineapple juice to make 1¼ cups liquid. Add to pork mixture.
5. Cook, covered, for 14 minutes, stirring once or twice during cooking period.
6. Stir in sweet and sour mix. Cook, covered, for 14 minutes, stirring occasionally during cooking period.
7. Cut pineapple slices in small pieces. Add to pork mixture with green pepper squares. Cook, covered, for 8 minutes, stirring once or twice during cooking period.
8. Remove from oven and let stand 5 minutes.
9. Serve with hot cooked rice or chow mein noodles.

Note: This dish tastes better when it is made early in the day and then heated at dinner time.

Barbecued Spareribs

4 servings

2 tablespoons cooking oil
½ cup minced onions
2 cans (8 ounces each) tomato sauce
2 tablespoons lemon juice
2 tablespoons brown sugar
1 tablespoon white sugar

2 teaspoons Worcestershire sauce
1 teaspoon prepared mustard
1 teaspoon salt
¼ teaspoon black pepper
1½ pounds spareribs

1. Put oil and onion in a 1-quart casserole. Cook, covered, for 3 minutes.
2. Add 2 tablespoons of water and remaining ingredients, except spareribs. Cover and cook for 7 minutes.
3. Cover and let stand.
4. Cut ribs apart between bones and place in a 3-quart casserole.
5. Cook, covered, for 25 minutes.
6. Pour off fat and juices. Cover ribs with ¾ cup of the barbecue sauce mixture.
7. Cook, uncovered, for 10 minutes.
8. Turn ribs over and cook again for 2 minutes.
9. Stir sauce and cook again for 13 minutes, stirring after 10 minutes.
10. Let stand a few minutes before serving.

Note: This recipe makes about 2½ cups sauce. Save remainder for other ribs or use on chicken or barbecued steak.

Baked Ham

10 to 12 servings

½ precooked smoked ham,
   about 4 pounds
1 can (4 ounces) pineapple slices,
   drained, juice reserved

¼ cup brown sugar
10 to 12 whole cloves

1. Score top of ham. Place in a baking dish to fit shape of ham.
2. Cook, covered with plastic wrap, for 32 minutes.
3. While ham is cooking combine 2 tablespoons pineapple juice and sugar. Remove ham and drain off liquid. Put pineapple slices on top of scored ham and stud with cloves. Drizzle pineapple juice mixture over top.
4. Cook, uncovered, for 16 to 17 minutes.
5. Cover with foil and let stand 20 minutes before carving.

Baked Ham Steak

2 servings

1 precooked ham steak, about 1
   pound

2 teaspoons brown sugar
½ teaspoon prepared mustard

1. Put ham steak in an 8-inch square baking dish.
2. Cook, covered with plastic wrap, for 9 minutes.
3. Remove from oven and drain off juices. Mix juices with brown sugar and mustard. Spread over top of steak.
4. Cook, uncovered, for 3 to 4 minutes.
5. Cover loosely and let stand 2 or 3 minutes before serving.

Scalloped Potatoes and Ham

4 servings

1½ cups milk
2 cups leftover pieces of baked ham
4 cups sliced potatoes
⅔ cup chopped onions
2 tablespoons all-purpose flour

1 teaspoon salt
⅛ teaspoon pepper
2 tablespoons butter or margarine
Paprika

1. Put milk in a 2-cup measure.
2. Cook, covered with waxed paper or plastic wrap, for 4 to 5 minutes, or just long enough to warm milk.
3. Put a layer of ham on bottom of a 2- or 3-quart glass casserole. Add a layer of potatoes and onion. Sprinkle with flour, salt, and pepper. Dot with butter. Add another layer of ham, potatoes, and onion. Pour hot milk over layers. Sprinkle with paprika.
4. Cook, covered, for about 30 minutes, or until potatoes are tender.
5. Uncover and cook again for 10 to 15 minutes.
6. Cover loosely with plastic wrap and let stand 2 minutes before serving.

Ham Casserole

4 servings

1½ cups diced cooked ham
2 tablespoons chopped onion
⅛ teaspoon tarragon
2 tablespoons butter or margarine
1 can (10½ ounces) condensed cream
  of chicken soup, undiluted

1½ cups cooked narrow egg noodles
½ cup cooked French-style green
  beans
2 tablespoons buttered bread crumbs

1. Combine ham, onion, tarragon, and butter in a 1½-quart casserole.
2. Cook, covered, for 3 to 4 minutes, or just long enough to melt butter and cook onion a little.
3. Add chicken soup, egg noodles, green beans, and ½ cup water. Toss lightly.
4. Cook, covered, for 10 to 12 minutes, or until piping hot. Stir once during cooking period.
5. Top with crumbs. Cover and let stand 2 to 3 minutes.

Bacon

8 strips

8 slices bacon

1. Separate bacon strips and lay 4 slices in an oblong baking dish on 2 layers of paper towels. Cover with 1 piece of paper towel. Place 4 more slices bacon on towel. Cover with towel.
2. Cook for 10 to 12 minutes, or to the desired degree of crispness.

Note: Cooking bacon in the microwave oven has more variables than almost any other food. Cooking time depends on the thickness of the slice, the amount of fat in the bacon, and the desired degree of crispness. It may be advisable to cook it the first time at the times suggested here, and thereafter cook it according to your own findings.

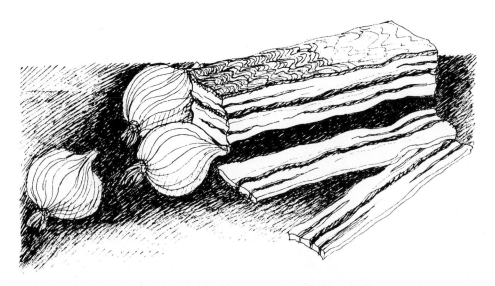

Poultry

Frozen whole chickens and turkeys can be successfully thawed in the microwave oven—just make sure to rotate the bird often. Allow the fowl to rest in between periods in the oven. Cover spots that begin to cook with bits of aluminum foil so that when the bird is cooked you will not have overdone spots. When roasting a bird, check for doneness by removing the bird from the oven and inserting the thermometer. If the temperature is 20° below the final temperature desired, it is time to let the bird stand— it will finish cooking out of the oven.

When cooking chicken parts, put the larger pieces of chicken on the outer edges of the dish and the smaller pieces in the center, so that all pieces will cook evenly.

Roast Chicken with Stuffing

4 to 6 servings

1 roasting chicken, about 5 pounds Salt to taste
½ package (7 ounces) stuffing mix

1. Wash chicken. Reserve giblets and neck and use for chicken stock.
2. Prepare stuffing mix according to package directions.
3. Sprinkle inside of cavity with salt. Fill cavity and neck opening with stuffing. Secure with toothpicks. Tie legs together loosely. Tie wings to body with string. Cover ends of the legs, the tail, and the wings with small pieces of aluminum foil.
4. Place inverted saucers in a 2-quart oblong baking dish. Place chicken breast-side down on saucers. Brush with butter. Cook, uncovered, for 30 minutes.
5. Remove chicken from dish and turn over so that breast side is up. Remove pieces of foil from chicken. Brush with butter. Cover with a piece of waxed paper.
6. Cook for about 30 minutes, or until a meat thermometer registers 180°.
7. Cover loosely with foil and let stand 10 to 15 minutes before carving. During this time the thermometer will rise to 195°, the proper temperature for cooked fowl.

Cooking Time for Roast Chicken

12 minutes per pound

General method:
Compute time before starting to cook. Cook half the time breast-side down, then invert the chicken and cook the remainder of time breast-side up.

To thaw frozen chicken:

1 frozen broiler-fryer chicken, split in half

Place chicken halves in an oblong casserole. Following the steps on the chart below, heat for given amounts of time. Once chicken is thawed it should be cooked immediately, as in the thawing process some of it may already have begun to cook.

1. Heat 4 minutes. Let stand 1 minute.
2. Heat 2 minutes. Let stand 1 minute.
3. Heat 2 minutes. Let stand 1 minute.
4. Heat 1 minute. Let stand 1 minute.
5. Heat 1 minute. Let stand 1 minute.

Chicken Balkan

4 servings

½ cup butter or margarine
1 broiler-fryer chicken, cut in serving pieces
1 onion, sliced
⅓ cup dry sherry

½ cup tomato juice
1 teaspoon paprika
1 teaspoon salt
Freshly ground pepper to taste

1. Place butter in an 8-inch square baking dish. Cook, uncovered, for about 1 minute, or just until butter melts.
2. Cut large pieces of chicken in half. Put in baking dish and turn so that all pieces are coated with melted butter. Place breasts in center of dish and surround with remaining pieces of chicken. Sprinkle onion slices on top.
3. Cook, uncovered, for 6 to 7 minutes.
4. Combine remaining ingredients with ½ cup water. Pour over chicken.
5. Cook, covered, for about 40 minutes, or until chicken is fork-tender.
6. Serve with rice pilaf.

Chicken Cacciatore

4 servings

¼ cup cooking oil
1 broiler-fryer chicken, cut in serving pieces
1 medium onion, coarsely chopped
1 clove garlic, minced
1 medium green pepper, seeded and coarsely chopped

1¼ teaspoons salt
⅛ teaspoon pepper
½ bay leaf
1 can (16 ounces) tomatoes
2 tablespoons dry white wine
Chopped parsley

1. Pour oil into an 8-inch square baking dish. Cut large pieces of chicken in half. Put in baking dish and turn so that all pieces are coated with oil. Place breasts in center and surround with other pieces of chicken. Sprinkle onion and garlic on top of chicken. Cook for 5 minutes.
2. Combine green pepper, salt, pepper, bay leaf, tomatoes, and wine. Stir with a fork and mash tomatoes into small pieces. Pour over top of chicken.
3. Cook, covered, for about 40 minutes, or until chicken is fork-tender.
4. Garnish with parsley and serve with cooked spaghetti.

To thaw a turkey:

If you have the time, you may thaw turkey according to package directions. If you are not cooking the turkey immediately this is advisable, as turkey will cook somewhat when thawed in the microwave oven.
1. Place turkey in plastic wrap in baking dish. Heat for 1½ to 2 minutes per pound, turning turkey over twice during cooking period.
2. Remove from oven and let stand 10 to 15 minutes to allow heat to penetrate turkey. Remove plastic wrap and metal staple that is used to hold down legs in some turkeys. Remove bag of giblets from turkey.
3. Heat for 1½ to 2 minutes per pound, turning turkey 2 or 3 times during cooking period. Check appearance and cover any brown spots with small pieces of aluminum foil.
4. Remove from oven and let stand 10 to 15 minutes to allow heat to penetrate turkey.
5. Heat turkey for about 1 minute per pound, turning turkey twice during cooking period. Be sure to cover any browned spots with small pieces of aluminum foil.

FOLLOWING PAGES: Left, *Chicken Cacciatore, page 63;* right, *Turkey Divan, page 67.*

6. Remove from oven and let stand 10 to 15 minutes. Insert a meat thermometer into breast of turkey. Thermometer should insert easily and should read 32° or higher.
7. If turkey has not thawed, heat again for about 1 minute per pound.
8. Let stand. Stuff and cook according to directions.

Note: Total thawing time is about 1½ to 2 hours for a 10-pound turkey.

Roast Turkey

1. Select a turkey between 8 and 12 pounds. A large bird can be cooked in the oven, if you can easily get it in and out of the oven when it is raised on saucers out of the drippings, with both breast-side up and breast-side down. A smaller bird is easier to maneuver and will not require any forcing.
2. Remove giblets and neck from turkey and rinse body cavity with water. Cook giblets and neck on top of the range in a conventional manner and use the broth for gravy or soup.
3. Pat turkey dry with paper towels. If stuffing is desired, stuff main cavity and neck cavity with desired stuffing. Secure neck skin and body opening with wooden skewers. Tie wings to body loosely with string. Tie legs together, loosely. Cover wings and legs with small pieces of foil.
4. Place inverted saucers or small casserole lids in the bottom of a 2- or 3-quart baking dish, depending on the size of the turkey. Turkey should not extend over sides of dish. Place turkey breast-side down on saucers.
5. Cook, uncovered, for half the allotted cooking time. (Compute time from the following table before you start cooking.) Remove turkey and turn breast-side up. Remove foil pieces. Brush with melted butter.
6. Continue cooking for remaining half of cooking time. During last half of cooking time watch turkey carefully. If it develops brown spots, this indicates overcooking; these spots should be covered with a small piece of aluminum foil to prevent further overcooking.
7. Remove turkey and insert a meat thermometer in the heavy part of the thigh or in the heavy part of the breast, making sure that it does not touch the bone. The thermometer should register about 170°, 10° to 15° lower than the final temperature. Cover turkey with foil and let stand about 20 minutes to bring temperature up to 185° and to make carving easier.

Cooking Time for Turkey

13 to 15 minutes per pound

Note: On newer meat thermometers required cooking temperatures are lower than on old thermometers. This may change cooking time.

Do not use the meat thermometer in oven while cooking. Insert when turkey is out of the oven. If turkey needs additional cooking time, remove thermometer and reinsert when turkey is removed from oven for the second time. Initial thermometer rise is very fast, so if it needs more time this will not take long.

Due to the long cooking time, the turkey will be browned, but the skin will not be crisp. If crisp skin is desired, reduce cooking time by about 30 seconds per pound. Crisp skin is obtained by baking about 15 minutes in a 450° conventional oven.

Turkey Tetrazzini
6 servings

4 ounces thin spaghetti
3 tablespoons butter or margarine
1 can (4 ounces) sliced mushrooms, drained
⅓ cup finely minced onions
3 tablespoons all-purpose flour
2 cups chicken broth or milk

½ cup light cream
¼ cup dry vermouth
1 teaspoon salt
Dash of white pepper
¾ cup grated Parmesan cheese, divided
2 cups diced cooked turkey

1. Cook spaghetti according to package directions. Drain immediately and rinse in cold water to stop cooking. Reserve.
2. Place butter in a 3-quart casserole. Add mushrooms and onion.
3. Cook, covered, for 3 to 4 minutes, or until onions are soft.
4. Add flour and mix to form a smooth paste.
5. Cook, covered, for 1 minute.
6. Stir in chicken broth, cream, vermouth, salt, pepper, and ¼ cup Parmesan cheese. Blend well.
7. Cook, uncovered, for 5 to 6 minutes, or until mixture comes to a boil and thickens. Stir once during cooking period.
8. Add cooked spaghetti, turkey, and remainder of cheese. Toss lightly.
9. Cook, covered, for 9 minutes, or until mixture is piping hot.
10. Let stand for about 5 minutes, before serving.

Note: Chicken or ham may be substituted for the turkey.

Turkey Divan
4 to 6 servings

1 bunch broccoli, cooked
8 to 12 slices cooked turkey breast
2 cups white sauce (see page 108)

¼ cup grated Parmesan cheese
¼ cup grated Gruyere cheese

1. Place cooked broccoli in a baking dish with flower ends at ends of dish. Cover center of stalks with slices of cooked turkey.
2. Prepare white sauce, and while it is still warm add the cheeses. Stir until well blended. Pour over top of turkey. Sprinkle with additional Parmesan cheese if desired.
3. Cook, covered with plastic wrap or waxed paper, for 9 to 10 minutes, or until turkey is piping hot.

Fish

Cooking fish in the microwave oven is one of the greatest time- and flavor-savers. Fish virtually cooks itself—the only trick is to be sure that it is not overcooked. Cook just until the fish flakes easily when tested with a fork—this can be done often during cooking time. Then remove from the oven and let stand for a time, because it continues to cook while standing. Shellfish should be watched even more carefully because it toughens very rapidly if overcooked.

OPPOSITE: *Stuffed Bass, page 70.*

Stuffed Bass

4 to 6 servings

1 whole bass, cleaned, about 3 pounds
2 cups fresh bread cubes
1 tablespoon melted butter or margarine
Salt and pepper to taste

1 tablespoon chopped parsley
1 teaspoon lemon juice
3 slices bacon

1. Wash fish in cold water. Pat dry with paper towels.
2. Combine bread cubes, butter, salt and pepper, parsley, and lemon juice. Toss lightly. Stuff cavity of fish. Close with toothpicks or tie with string.
3. Place fish in an oblong baking dish. Place bacon slices on fish.
4. Cook, covered, for 8 to 10 minutes.
5. Drain liquid and fat from bottom of dish. Cook, covered with paper towels, for about 8 minutes, or until fish flakes easily when tested with a fork.
6. Let fish stand covered with paper towels 5 minutes before serving.

Halibut Steaks

4 servings

2 halibut steaks, about ¾ inch thick
½ lemon
1 egg, beaten
½ can (10¾ ounces) condensed cream of celery soup

2 tablespoons milk
2 tablespoons grated Parmesan cheese, divided
2 tablespoons fine dry bread crumbs
2 teaspoons melted butter or margarine

1. Wipe fish with a damp paper towel. Cut each steak in 2 portions. Place in an 8-inch square baking dish. Squeeze lemon over top of fish. Set aside.
2. In a 2-cup measure beat together egg, soup, milk, and 1 tablespoon cheese.
3. Cook, covered, for 2 minutes. Remove and stir well to melt cheese.
4. Pour soup mixture over steaks. Combine bread crumbs and melted butter and sprinkle over top of fish. Top with remaining 1 tablespoon cheese.
5. Cook, covered, for 10 minutes, or until fish flakes when tested with a fork.

Filet of Sole Almondine

4 servings

½ cup slivered almonds
½ cup butter or margarine
1 pound fresh or frozen fillet of sole
½ teaspoon salt

⅛ teaspoon pepper
1 teaspoon chopped parsley
1 tablespoon lemon juice

1. Place almonds and butter in an 8-inch square baking dish.
2. Cook, uncovered, for 6 to 7 minutes, or until almonds and butter are golden brown. Remove almonds with a slotted spoon and set aside.
3. Arrange sole in dish with butter, turning to coat both sides of fish. Sprinkle with salt, pepper, parsley, and lemon juice.
4. Cook, covered with waxed paper or plastic wrap, for 8 minutes.
5. Remove waxed paper. Sprinkle fish with toasted almonds. Cook, covered, for 2 minutes, or until fish flakes easily when tested with a fork.
6. Let stand 1 to 2 minutes before serving. To serve, garnish with lemon wedges and sprigs of parsley.

Tuna-Spinach Casserole

4 servings

1 package (10 ounces) raw spinach
1 can (7 ounces) solid pack tuna
1 can (4 ounces) sliced mushrooms
2 tablespoons lemon juice
3 tablespoons butter or margarine, divided

1 tablespoon minced onion
2 tablespoons all-purpose flour
½ teaspoon salt
⅛ teaspoon pepper
1 egg, lightly beaten

1. Rinse spinach in fresh, cold water. Drain well. Break in pieces, removing tough center stems. Put in a 2-quart casserole.
2. Cook, covered, for 7 to 8 minutes, until spinach is limp. Drain well and set aside.
3. Drain tuna and set aside.
4. Drain mushrooms, reserving liquid. Put mushroom liquid in a 1-cup measure. Add lemon juice and enough water to make 1 cup of liquid.
5. Put 2 tablespoons of the butter in a 1-quart casserole. Cook for 30 seconds, or just long enough to melt butter.
6. Add onion, flour, salt, and pepper. Cook, uncovered, for 1 minute.
7. Stir in mushroom liquid. Cook, uncovered, for 4 to 4½ minutes, or until thick, stirring occasionally during cooking time.
8. Add a small amount of sauce to egg, beat well, and return to hot sauce. Stir mushrooms into sauce.
9. Put drained spinach in a 2- to 3-quart casserole. Break tuna in big chunks and place over top of spinach. Pour sauce over top. Dot with remaining 1 tablespoon of butter.
10. Cook, uncovered, for 9 to 11 minutes. Let stand covered with waxed paper 3 to 4 minutes before serving.

Steamed Clams

2 servings

1 quart steamer clams

Melted butter or margarine

1. Scrub clams with a stiff brush to remove all sand and grit. Discard all clams that are even the least bit open.
2. Put scrubbed clams in a 2-quart casserole. Add 2 tablespoons water.
3. Cook, covered, for 13 minutes, or until clam shells are all open and clams are cooked. Discard clams with closed shells.
4. Serve clams in flat bowls. Divide clam liquid into custard cups and fill a second set of cups with melted butter. Remove clams from shells, dip in clam liquid, and then in butter.
5. Drink clam broth when clams have been eaten.

FOLLOWING PAGES: Left, *Filet of Sole Almondine,* page 70; right, *Tuna Crunch,* page 74.

Tuna Crunch

4 servings

1 cup thinly sliced celery
¼ cup chopped onion
2 tablespoons butter or margarine
1 can (7 ounces) tuna fish

1 can (10¾ ounces) cream of
mushroom soup, undiluted
1 can (3 ounces) chow mein noodles
½ cup coarsely chopped cashews

1. Combine celery, onion, and butter in a 1-quart casserole. Cook, uncovered, for 6 to 7 minutes, stirring once during cooking time.
2. Drain tuna and flake with a fork. Add to onion mixture with soup, ⅔ can of noodles, and cashews. Toss lightly.
3. Cook, covered, for 4 minutes.
4. Stir mixture lightly. Top with remaining noodles. Cook, covered, for 6 to 7 minutes, or until piping hot.

Crab Meat in Shells

4 servings

1 tablespoon chopped parsley
1 tablespoon chopped green pepper
1 scallion, chopped, including green
top
1 can (4 ounces) sliced mushrooms and
pieces, well drained
1 teaspoon butter
1 can (10¾ ounces) condensed cream
of celery soup, undiluted

1 can (7½ ounces) crab meat
1 tablespoon lemon juice
1 tablespoon dry sherry
2 tablespoons dry bread crumbs
2 tablespoons grated Cheddar cheese
Paprika

1. Combine parsley, green pepper, scallion, mushrooms, and butter in a 1-quart casserole.
2. Cook, covered, for 4 to 5 minutes.
3. Add soup and blend well. Cook, covered, for 2 minutes.
4. Pick over crab meat and remove any bits of cartilage. Add to mixture with lemon juice and sherry. Divide mixture into 4 scallop shells. Combine bread crumbs and cheese. Spread over top of crab mixture. Sprinkle generously with paprika.
5. Cook 2 shells at a time for 9 minutes, rotating midway in cooking period.

Lobster Tails

4 servings

1 pound frozen lobster tails
1 teaspoon lemon juice

¼ cup butter or margarine
¼ teaspoon grated lemon peel

1. Place frozen lobster tails in an 8-inch square baking dish. Sprinkle with lemon juice. Cook for 6 minutes to thaw lobster.
2. Cut away soft shell-like surface on underside of tail with a sharp knife or scissors. Insert wooden skewers into each lobster tail to keep flat while cooking. Drain liquid from dish and arrange lobster in dish shell side down.

3. Combine butter and lemon peel in a small custard cup. Cook for 30 seconds until melted.
4. Brush tails with butter mixture.
5. Cook, covered, for 9 minutes, or until lobster meat turns pink.
6. Serve hot with melted butter and lemon wedges.

Scallops Poulette   4 servings

¼ cup butter or margarine
1 tablespoon minced onion
¼ cup flour
1 can (4 ounces) sliced mushrooms, drained
¼ cup dry vermouth
½ teaspoon salt

⅛ teaspoon pepper
1 pound bay scallops
1 bay leaf
2 teaspoons lemon juice
½ cup light cream
1 egg yolk
1 tablespoon chopped parsley

1. Combine butter and onion in a 2-quart casserole.
2. Cook, uncovered, for 4 minutes.
3. Stir in flour and blend well. Add mushrooms, wine, salt, pepper, scallops, bay leaf, and lemon juice. Toss together lightly.
4. Cook, covered, for 10 minutes, or until scallops are tender.
5. Remove bay leaf. Beat together cream and egg yolk. Add some hot liquid carefully to egg and blend well. Stir egg mixture carefully into hot casserole. Stir well.
6. Cook, covered, for 6 to 7 minutes, stirring twice during cooking period.
7. Sprinkle with parsley and serve.

Shrimp Creole   6 servings

3 tablespoons butter or margarine
½ cup chopped onions
½ cup chopped green pepper
½ cup diced celery
1 clove garlic, minced
1 can (1 pound) tomatoes, mashed
1 can (8 ounces) tomato sauce

1 tablespoon Worcestershire sauce
1½ teaspoons salt
1 teaspoon sugar
½ teaspoon chili powder
Dash of hot-pepper sauce
1 tablespoon cornstarch
1 pound cooked shrimp

1. Combine butter, onion, green pepper, celery, and garlic in a 2- or 3-quart casserole.
2. Cook for 4 minutes, covered, stirring once.
3. Add tomatoes, tomato sauce, Worcestershire, salt, sugar, chili powder, and hot-pepper sauce.
4. Cook, for 8 minutes, covered, stirring twice during cooking period.
5. Combine cornstarch with 2 teaspoons cold water. Stir into casserole.
6. Cook, uncovered, for 4 minutes, stirring once or twice.
7. Add shrimp. Cook, uncovered, for 3 minutes, or until shrimp is piping hot.
8. Serve with wild rice or plain boiled rice.

FOLLOWING PAGES: Left, *Steamed Clams, page 71;* right, *Shrimp Creole, page 75.*

Scallops Cacciatore

4 servings

1 medium onion, chopped	¼ cup dry white wine
1 medium green pepper, chopped	1¼ teaspoons salt
¼ cup salad oil	⅛ teaspoon pepper
1 can (1 pound) tomatoes, drained	2 bay leaves
1 pound bay scallops	2 tablespoons chopped parsley
1 can (8 ounces) tomato sauce	

1. Combine onion, green pepper, garlic, and oil in a 1½- to 2-quart casserole.
2. Cook for 4 minutes, covered, stirring once.
3. Mash tomatoes with a fork to break into small pieces. Add to casserole with scallops, tomato sauce, wine, salt, pepper, and bay leaves.
4. Cook, covered, 10 minutes or until scallops are tender.
5. Sprinkle with parsley. Serve with hot cooked rice, if desired.

Eggs, Pasta, and Cheese

Eggs and cheese require careful watching and cooking. Eggs cook so quickly that they can easily be overcooked in just seconds. Time them carefully. When baking or shirring eggs, it is wise to prick the yolk gently with the point of a very sharp knife—just enough to allow the steam to escape so that the yolks will not burst. Cheese that is overcooked by any method—conventional or microwave —will become rubbery. Undercook slightly, rather than overcook any cheese dish.

FOLLOWING PAGES: Left, *Eggs Benedict, page 82;* right, *Shirred Eggs, page 82; Sticky Buns, page 138.*

Poached Egg

1 serving

1 egg

1. Bring ⅓ cup water to a boil in a small custard cup, for 1 to 1½ minutes.
2. Carefully break egg into a small dish or saucer. Slide egg into boiling water.
3. Cook, tightly covered, for 1 minute. Keep covered and let stand 1 minute before serving.

Fried Egg

1 serving

1 teaspoon butter or margarine   **1 egg**

1. Place butter in a small custard cup or sauce dish. Cook for 1 minute, or just until melted.
2. Carefully break egg into dish. Cook, tightly covered, for about 1 minute. Keep covered and let stand 1 minute before serving.

Eggs Benedict

4 servings

¾ cup hollandaise sauce   **4 slices ham, ¼ to ½ inch thick**
2 English muffins, split and toasted   **4 poached eggs**

1. Prepare hollandaise sauce. Cover with a piece of waxed paper and set aside.
2. Place each muffin half on a paper plate and top each with 1 slice ham.
3. Cook, uncovered, 2 at a time, for 2 to 2½ minutes, or until ham is hot.
4. Top each with a poached egg. Cover with hollandaise sauce and serve immediately.

Shirred Eggs

1 serving

1 teaspoon butter or margarine   **2 eggs**

1. Melt butter in a ramekin or small cereal bowl for about 1 minute.
2. Break eggs carefully into ramekin or bowl. Cover tightly with plastic wrap.
3. Cook, covered, for 2½ to 3 minutes.
4. Remove and let stand 1 minute before serving. Serve with crisp bacon and buttered toast.

Welsh Rabbit on Toast

4 to 6 servings

4 teaspoons butter or margarine   **¼ teaspoon dry mustard**
4 cups (1 pound) shredded sharp   **¼ teaspoon cayenne**
** Cheddar cheese**   **2 eggs, lightly beaten**
¾ teaspoon Worcestershire sauce   **1 cup flat beer or ale, at room**
½ teaspoon salt   ** temperature**
½ teaspoon paprika

1. Melt butter in a 2-quart casserole or bowl, for about 3 minutes.
2. Add cheese, Worcestershire, salt, paprika, dry mustard, and cayenne. Mix thoroughly.
3. Cook, covered, for 5 minutes, stirring twice.
4. Stir a little of the hot cheese into beaten eggs. Return slowly to hot mixture and stir briskly. Gradually stir in beer and blend well.
5. Cook, covered, for 12 minutes, stirring at 4-minute intervals.
6. Remove from oven and beat briskly with a whisk to blend thoroughly.
7. Serve over crisp toasted French bread slices and garnish with tomatoes and crisp bacon slices.

Swiss Cheese Fondue   6 servings

4 cups shredded Swiss cheese	Dash of pepper
¼ cup all-purpose flour	2 cups dry white wine
¼ teaspoon salt	2 tablespoons Kirsch
¼ teaspoon nutmeg	1 loaf French bread, cut into cubes

1. In a 1½-quart dish or casserole combine cheese, flour, salt, nutmeg, and pepper. Toss lightly to coat cheese with flour. Stir in wine.
2. Cook, covered, for about 5 minutes, stirring during last 2 minutes of cooking time. Stir well after removing from oven to finish melting cheese.
3. If cheese is not all melted, return to oven for 1 minute.
4. Stir in Kirsch.
5. Serve immediately with cubes of French bread. Spear each cube of bread on a fondue fork; dip into fondue and eat immediately.
6. If fondue cools during eating time, return to oven for 1 minute to reheat.

Green Noodles   6 servings

¼ cup butter or margarine	1 cup diced sharp Cheddar cheese
¼ cup all-purpose flour	¼ cup grated Parmesan cheese
1 teaspoon salt	3 cups cooked green noodles
¼ teaspoon hot-pepper sauce	3 hard-cooked eggs, halved
2½ cups milk	

1. Put butter in a 1½-quart casserole.
2. Cook, covered, for 1½ minutes, or until butter is melted.
3. Remove and stir in flour, salt, and hot-pepper sauce to make a smooth paste.
4. Cook for 1 minute.
5. Gradually stir in milk. Cook, covered, for about 10 minutes, stirring occasionally during last half of cooking time.
6. Remove and stir briskly to make a smooth sauce. Add Cheddar cheese and Parmesan cheese and stir until cheese is melted. Add noodles and toss until well coated.
7. Cook, covered, for 7 to 8 minutes.
8. Top with egg halves. Cook, covered, for 4 minutes, or until piping hot.

FOLLOWING PAGES: Left, *Welsh Rabbit*, page 82; right, *Swiss Cheese Fondue*, page 83.

Manicotti

8 to 10 servings

1 package (8 ounces) manicotti
  noodles
1 package (1 pound) ricotta cheese
½ pound mozzarella cheese, grated
Parmesan cheese
3 tablespoons chopped parsley,
  divided
3 teaspoons sugar, divided
1 egg, lightly beaten

Salt and pepper to taste
2 sweet Italian sausages
1 clove garlic, minced
1 medium onion, minced
1 pound ground beef
1 can (12 ounces) tomatoes, mashed
1 can (16 ounces) tomato sauce
½ teaspoon basil

1. Cook manicotti noodles according to package directions for 12 minutes on conventional range. Drain and reserve.
2. Combine ricotta, mozzarella, 3 tablespoons Parmesan cheese, 1 tablespoon parsley, 2 teaspoons sugar, egg, and salt and pepper to taste. Blend well and reserve.
3. Remove sausage from casings. Crumble into a 2- or 3-quart casserole. Add garlic, onion, and 2 tablespoons chopped parsley.
4. Cook, covered, for about 4 minutes, stirring once during cooking time.
5. Crumble ground beef on top of sausage meat and toss lightly. Cook, covered, for 7 minutes, stirring and breaking meat up at least once during cooking time.
6. Add tomatoes, tomato sauce, basil, 1 teaspoon sugar, and salt and pepper to taste.
7. Cook, covered, for 15 minutes, stirring occasionally.
8. Pour a thin layer of meat sauce on the bottom of two 2-quart baking dishes or flat casseroles.
9. Fill cooked manicotti tubes with cheese mixture. Place 10 filled tubes close together in each casserole. Cover with remaining meat sauce.
10. Cook, covered tightly, for 30 minutes.
11. Remove cover, sprinkle top of casserole with ¼ cup grated Parmesan. Cook for 5 minutes, or just until cheese is melted.

Note: This recipe makes 2 casseroles. Use one immediately and freeze the second for later use.

Macaroni Goulash

6 to 8 servings

1 cup uncooked macaroni
1 pound ground beef
1 can (1 pound) tomato puree, or 1 can
  (1 pound) tomatoes packed in puree
½ teaspoon sugar

½ teaspoon basil
1 teaspoon salt
Pepper to taste
1 tablespoon chopped parsley

1. Cook macaroni on conventional range according to package directions. Set aside.

2. Crumble beef into a 2- or 3-quart casserole. Cook, uncovered, for 7 to 8 minutes, stirring once to break up meat.
3. Add puree, sugar, basil, salt, pepper to taste, and parsley. Stir in macaroni.
4. Cook, covered, for about 12 minutes, stirring once during cooking time.
5. Let stand, covered, about 3 to 4 minutes before serving.

Variation: To stretch amount, use 1 can (1 pound 12 ounces) tomato puree and increase macaroni to 1½ cups.

Noodles and Chicken
4 to 6 servings

1½ cups broken egg noodles
2 to 3 cups cut-up cooked chicken
  or turkey
1 cup chicken stock
½ cup milk

½ teaspoon salt
⅛ teaspoon pepper
1 cup shredded Cheddar cheese
¼ cup sliced stuffed green olives

1. In a 1½- or 2-quart casserole combine noodles, chicken, chicken stock, milk, salt, and pepper. Stir lightly.
2. Cook, covered, for 23 to 26 minutes, or until noodles are tender.
3. Stir in cheese and olives. Let stand until cheese is melted before serving.

Spitzer's Sunday-Night Special
4 to 6 servings

1 can (7 ounces) green chilies
1 cup coarsely crushed corn chips
Meat (optional)
  2 mild Italian sausages, cooked
    and broken up, or
  ½ pound ground chuck, cooked, or
  1 cup ground cooked pork or ham
½ cup cottage cheese or ricotta

4 ounces Monterey Jack cheese, cut in
  strips
2 eggs
1 cup milk
½ teaspoon salt
½ cup grated Cheddar or Parmesan
  cheese

1. Wash and dry chilies. Remove any remaining seeds. Cut into strips 1 inch wide.
2. Put half the corn chips in bottom of an 8-inch round cake pan. Arrange about one-third of the chilies on top of corn chips. Place meat, if desired, on top of chilies. Dot cottage cheese on top of meat. Add another third of the chilies. Arrange Monterey Jack cheese over top of chilies. Arrange remaining chilies on top of cheese.
3. Beat together eggs, milk, and salt. Pour over top of mixture in casserole. Sprinkle top with Cheddar or Parmesan cheese. Sprinkle remaining corn chips on top of cheese.
4. Cook, uncovered, for 16 to 18 minutes, or until custard is set.
5. Remove from oven and let stand, covered, for about 5 minutes.

87

FOLLOWING PAGES: Left, *Spaghetti Sauce;* right, *Macaroni and Cheese;* page 91.

Swiss and Onion Pie

6 to 8 slices

4 slices bacon
1 large onion, thinly sliced
1 tablespoon butter or margarine
1 9-inch baked pastry shell
½ pound Swiss cheese, grated

1 tablespoon all-purpose flour
3 eggs, lightly beaten
1 cup milk
½ teaspoon salt
⅛ teaspoon pepper

1. Place bacon slices on 2 paper towels. Cover with another paper towel. Cook for 5 to 6 minutes, or until almost crisp. Reserve bacon.
2. Combine onion and butter in a 1-quart casserole.
3. Cook, covered, for 5 to 6 minutes, or until onion is limp.
4. Place cooked onion in prebaked pastry shell. Toss together cheese and flour and sprinkle over onion. Beat together eggs, milk, salt, and pepper. Pour over cheese.
5. Cook for 17 minutes, rotating every 2 minutes.
6. Place bacon strips on top of pie. Cook for 5 to 6 minutes, or until custard is almost set. Let stand 10 to 15 minutes to finish cooking.

Mock Manicotti

10 to 12 servings

1 package (8 ounces) wide egg noodles
1 pound ground beef
1 can (16 ounces) tomato sauce
1 pound creamed cottage cheese
¼ cup dairy sour cream

1 scallion, chopped, including top
1 tablespoon chopped green pepper
1 tablespoon chopped parsley
Salt and pepper to taste
2 tablespoons melted butter or margarine

1. Cook egg noodles on conventional range according to package directions. Reserve.
2. Crumble ground beef into a 3-quart casserole. Cook, uncovered, for 7 to 8 minutes, stirring occasionally to break up meat.
3. Stir in tomato sauce. Cook, covered, for 7 to 8 minutes.
4. Combine cottage cheese, sour cream, scallion, green pepper, parsley, and salt and pepper to taste.
5. Put half the cooked noodles in the bottom of a 3-quart casserole. Cover noodles with cheese mixture. Cover with remaining noodles. Pour melted butter over top of noodles. Top with ground beef mixture.
6. Cook, covered, for 10 to 15 minutes, or until mixture is piping hot.

Note: This mixture may be prepared in 2 small casseroles. Heat one for dinner and freeze the other for later use.

Macaroni Quickie

4 servings

½ pound ground beef
1 cup uncooked elbow macaroni
1 medium onion, chopped
1 can (8 ounces) tomato sauce
⅓ cup catsup

Pinch of sugar
½ teaspoon salt
¼ teaspoon pepper
¼ teaspoon chili powder

1. Combine all ingredients with 1½ cups water in a 2- to 2½-quart casserole. Blend well.
2. Cook, covered tightly, for 25 to 30 minutes, or until macaroni is tender. Stir occasionally during cooking time.
3. Let stand 4 to 5 minutes before serving to blend flavors.

Spaghetti Sauce   about 2 quarts

½ pound ground beef	2 teaspoons salt
½ cup chopped onions	2 teaspoons oregano
2 cloves garlic, minced	¼ teaspoon basil
1 can (28 ounces) tomatoes	¼ teaspoon ground thyme
2 cans (6 ounces each) tomato paste	Freshly ground pepper to taste

1. Crumble beef into a 3-quart casserole. Add onion and garlic.
2. Cook, uncovered, for about 9 minutes, stirring at least twice to break up meat.
3. Add remaining ingredients. Break up whole tomatoes with a fork or potato masher.
4. Cook, covered, for 25 to 30 minutes, or until mixture is well blended and slightly thickened.
5. Cover and let stand for 5 to 10 minutes.
6. Serve piping hot over hot cooked spaghetti.

Macaroni and Cheese   4 servings

1½ cups uncooked macaroni	Freshly ground pepper to taste
2 tablespoons butter or margarine	1 cup milk
2 tablespoons all-purpose flour	2 cups shredded sharp Cheddar
¼ teaspoon salt	cheese, divided
½ teaspoon Worcestershire sauce	¼ cup cracker crumbs
½ teaspoon prepared mustard	Tomato slices (optional)

1. Cook macaroni on conventional range according to package directions. Drain and set aside.
2. Melt butter in a 2-quart casserole for 30 seconds.
3. Stir in flour, salt, Worcestershire, mustard, and pepper. Cook, uncovered, for 1 minute.
4. Gradually stir in milk. Cook, uncovered, for 4 to 4½ minutes, stirring occasionally during last half of cooking time.
5. Stir in 1½ cups shredded cheese and continue stirring until cheese is melted. If cheese is not melted, cook for 30 seconds, or just until cheese is melted.
6. Stir cooked macaroni into sauce. Top with remaining cheese and cracker crumbs, and with tomato slices if desired.
7. Cook, uncovered, for 5 to 6 minutes, or until cheese is melted and macaroni is piping hot.
8. Let stand about 4 minutes before serving.

Vegetables

Because vegetables are cooked in very little water, in a tightly covered dish, and for a short length of time, they retain more nutrients and, most important, keep their color and flavor better than with conventional cooking. Vegetables should be crisp-cooked, almost Chinese style, because—as most foods do—they will continue to cook after they are removed from the microwave oven. In order to assure even cooking, vegetables should be cut in uniform pieces and stirred during the cooking time.

OPPOSITE: *Harvard Beets, page 99.*

Artichoke Hearts

3 to 4 servings

Place 1 10-ounce package frozen artichoke hearts in a 1-quart casserole. Add 2 to 3 tablespoons water. Cook, covered, for 10 to 11 minutes, or until artichoke hearts are tender. Stir once during cooking time.

Artichoke Hearts with Mushrooms

3 to 4 servings

1 package (10 ounces) frozen artichoke hearts	½ teaspoon lemon juice
	Salt and pepper
1 can (4 ounces) sliced mushrooms	Onion salt
1½ teaspoons cornstarch	Garlic salt
2 tablespoons dry sherry	1 tablespoon chopped parsley
2 tablespoons butter or margarine	

1. Cook artichoke hearts according to preceding directions. Set aside.
2. Drain mushrooms, reserving liquid.
3. Combine cornstarch, sherry, butter, lemon juice, and mushroom liquid in a 1-quart bowl.
4. Cook, uncovered, for 1 to 1½ minutes, or until mixture is thickened and clear. Blend well.
5. Season to taste with salt, pepper, onion salt, and garlic salt. Stir in parsley. Cut artichoke hearts in half and add them, along with the mushrooms. Stir gently.
6. Heat, covered, for 4 to 5 minutes, until mixture is piping hot.

Asparagus

3 to 4 servings

Buy straight, green, crisp stalks with close, compact heads. Select stalks of uniform size so that they will all cook in the same length of time.

Break off each stalk as far down as it will snap easily. Scrub lightly with a soft brush and remove scales with a knife, or remove scales and thinly pare the stalks with a vegetable peeler. The latter method is recommended if stalks are very thick and tough and if the asparagus is very sandy.

Lay 1 pound asparagus spears in a flat dish. Add ¼ cup water. Cook, covered, for 9 to 11 minutes, or until asparagus is tender.

Frozen Asparagus

2 to 3 servings

Place 1 10-ounce package asparagus spears, icy side up, in a 1-quart casserole. Cook, covered, for 10 to 11 minutes. Move asparagus in center of casserole to outer edges of casserole once during cooking time.

Asparagus Vinaigrette Bundles

5 to 6 servings

2 dozen fresh asparagus spears
6 tablespoons cooking oil
3 tablespoons vinegar
⅛ teaspoon hot-pepper sauce

½ teaspoon sugar
¼ teaspoon salt
1 small onion, sliced
Pimiento strips

1. Cook asparagus spears 10 to 11 minutes. Cool. Place in a shallow dish.
2. Combine remaining ingredients, except pimiento, and blend well. Pour over asparagus and let stand in refrigerator several hours or overnight.
3. Wrap pimiento strips around 4 or 5 asparagus spears. Serve as a cold vegetable or place on lettuce cups and serve as a salad.

Green Beans

3 to 4 servings

Choose crisp, brightly colored, fully formed pods. Wash beans. Remove ends and cut or break 1 pound beans into pieces of uniform size. Place beans in a 1-quart casserole. Add ⅓ cup water. Cook, covered, for 19 to 21 minutes, or until beans are done to the desired degree of tenderness. Season to taste.

Frozen Green Beans

2 to 3 servings

Place a 10-ounce package of frozen green beans in a 1-quart casserole. Add 3 tablespoons water. Cook, covered, for about 14 minutes, or until done.

Peppered Beans

3 to 4 servings

1 pound green beans
2 tablespoons olive oil
½ sweet red or green pepper, seeded
    and cut in slivers

¼ cup blanched slivered almonds
Salt and pepper to taste

1. Cook beans according to preceding directions. Cover and let stand.
2. Combine oil, red or green pepper, and almonds in a 1-quart casserole.
3. Cook, uncovered, for about 5 minutes, or until peppers are limp.
4. Toss with green beans. Season to taste with salt and pepper.

Green Beans Italian

6 servings

2 packages (10 ounces each) frozen
green beans
1 small onion, thinly sliced

¾ cup bottled Italian dressing
3 strips cooked bacon

1. Place green beans in a 1½-quart casserole or saucepan, icy side up.
2. Cook, covered, for about 13 minutes, or until almost tender, stirring once during cooking time.
3. Add onion and Italian dressing.
4. Cook, covered, for about 5 minutes, or until beans are just crisply tender.
5. Serve hot, topped with crumbled cooked bacon.

Green Beans Piquant

3 to 4 servings

1 pound green beans
2 tablespoons butter or margarine
1 teaspoon prepared mustard

1 tablespoon Worcestershire sauce
Salt and pepper to taste

1. Cook beans according to directions on page 95.
2. When beans are tender, add remaining ingredients and toss lightly until butter is melted and beans are well coated with mixture.

Savory Green Beans

3 to 4 servings

1 pound green beans
2 tablespoons olive oil
1 clove garlic, minced
1 teaspoon catsup

1 teaspoon Worcestershire sauce
¼ teaspoon savory
Salt to taste

1. Cook green beans according to directions. Cover and keep warm.
2. Combine olive oil and garlic in a 1-quart serving bowl.
3. Cook, uncovered, for 2½ to 3 minutes, or until garlic is tender.
4. Add catsup, Worcestershire, and savory. Add hot beans and toss lightly. Season to taste with salt.

96

OPPOSITE: *Stuffed Eggplant, Stuffed Green Peppers, page 102, Eggs in Nests, page 103.*

Frozen Lima Beans

3 to 4 servings

Place 1 10-ounce package frozen baby lima beans in a 1-quart casserole. Add ¼ cup water. Cook, covered, for 15 to 16 minutes, or until tender. Stir once during cooking period.

Lima Beans Parmesan

3 to 4 servings

1 package (10 ounces) frozen baby lima beans	1 clove garlic
¼ cup chicken bouillon	Salt and pepper to taste
1 bay leaf	Grated Parmesan cheese

1. Place lima beans in a 1½-quart casserole. Add chicken bouillon, bay leaf, and garlic.
2. Cook, covered, for 15 to 16 minutes until beans are tender.
3. Remove bay leaf and garlic. Season to taste with salt and pepper. Serve with Parmesan cheese sprinkled on top of beans.

Beets

4 servings

Wash well and cut stems and root ends from 1 bunch (4 to 5 medium) beets. Place in a deep 2½-quart mixing bowl with water to cover. Cover with plastic wrap. Cook for 30 to 35 minutes, or until beets can be easily pierced with the point of a sharp knife. Drain and slip off skins. Serve whole or sliced.

Beets in Orange Sauce

4 servings

1 can (1 pound) diced beets	¼ cup orange juice
1 tablespoon cornstarch	2 tablespoons lemon juice
¾ teaspoon salt	½ teaspoon grated orange peel
1½ tablespoons sugar	1 tablespoon butter or margarine

1. Drain beets, reserving liquid. Pour liquid into a measuring cup and add enough water to make ½ cup liquid.
2. Combine cornstarch, salt, sugar, and orange juice in a 1-quart bowl. Stir in beet liquid.
3. Cook, uncovered, for about 6 minutes, stirring occasionally, or until mixture comes to a boil and is clear.
4. Add lemon juice, orange peel, and butter. Stir to melt butter. Add beets.
5. Cook, uncovered, for 4 to 5 minutes, or until beets are piping hot.

Harvard Beets

4 servings

1 can (1 pound) diced or sliced beets	½ teaspoon salt
¼ cup sugar	Freshly ground pepper to taste
1 tablespoon cornstarch	¼ cup vinegar

1. Drain beets, reserving liquid. Pour beet liquid into a 1-cup measure and add enough water to make 1 cup of liquid.
2. Combine sugar, cornstarch, salt, pepper, and vinegar in a 1-quart casserole or bowl. Stir in beet liquid.
3. Cook, uncovered, for about 7 minutes, stirring occasionally, until mixture thickens and is clear.
4. Add beets and stir lightly.
5. Cook, covered, for about 5 minutes, or until beets are piping hot.

Pickled Beets

2 cups

1 can (1 pound) sliced beets	⅓ cup vinegar
⅓ cup sugar	1 teaspoon pickling spice

1. Drain beets, reserving ⅓ cup of the beet liquid. Place beets in a 1-quart casserole with sugar, beet liquid, and vinegar. Tie pickling spice in a small square of cheesecloth and add to beets.
2. Cook, covered, for 6 to 7 minutes, or until mixture comes to a boil.
3. Cool and remove bag of spices. Refrigerate up to 2 weeks.

Broccoli

4 servings

Peel stems off a bunch of broccoli, about 1½ pounds. Remove leaves and cut off a slice from tough bottom. Split stems about 1-inch up to make for faster, more even cooking. Place in a 1½-quart casserole with the split stem ends arranged toward the outside of the dish. Add ¼ cup water. Cook, covered, for 12 to 13 minutes, or until broccoli is tender.

Frozen Broccoli

2 to 3 servings

Place a 10-ounce package of frozen broccoli in a 1-quart casserole, icy side up. Cook, covered, for 12 to 13 minutes, rearranging broccoli after first 5 minutes of cooking.

Broccoli Indienne

3 to 4 servings

1 bunch broccoli, about 1½ pounds
⅓ cup chicken bouillon
1 bay leaf
¼ teaspoon thyme

2 tablespoons lemon juice
1 tablespoon butter or margarine
Salt to taste

1. Wash broccoli. Cut off tough bottom stalks and discard. Remove leaves and peel tough skin from stalks. Cut stems in chunks, leaving flowerets intact.
2. Place stem chunks on sides and flowerets in center of a 1½-quart casserole. Add chicken bouillon, bay leaf, and thyme.
3. Cook, covered, for 12 to 13 minutes, or until tender.
4. Discard bay leaf and add lemon juice and butter. Toss lightly and season to taste with salt.

Frozen Brussels Sprouts

3 to 4 servings

Place 1 package (10 ounces) frozen brussels sprouts in a 1-quart casserole. Add ¼ cup water. Cook, covered, for 13 to 14 minutes, or until tender, stirring once or twice during cooking period.

Cabbage

3 to 4 servings

Select a fresh-leafed head that is heavy for its size. New cabbage should be very green in color, though rather loose-leafed. Mature heads are paler in color and very solid. Red cabbage makes a pleasant change and is selected and cooked the same way as green cabbage.

Remove outer leaves of cabbage and wash whole head under running water. Cut in quarters. Remove most of core.

With a very sharp knife, thinly slice ½ medium head of cabbage into medium shreds. Place in a 1½-quart casserole with 2 tablespoons water. Cook, covered, for 9 to 11 minutes, stirring once. Season to taste.

Norwegian Cabbage

3 to 4 servings

½ head cabbage
½ cup dairy sour cream

½ teaspoon caraway seeds
Salt and pepper to taste

1. Shred cabbage. Cook about 9 to 11 minutes. Drain.
2. Toss lightly with sour cream and caraway seeds. Season to taste with salt and pepper. Serve hot.

100

OPPOSITE: *Baked Potatoes, page 107; Cauliflower and Tomatoes, page 105.*

Sweet and Sour Cabbage

4 to 6 servings

4 cups shredded cabbage
2 apples, peeled, cored, and finely
  chopped
¼ cup brown sugar

1 teaspoon salt
⅛ teaspoon pepper
½ cup butter
¼ cup vinegar

1. Place cabbage in a 1½-quart glass casserole. Combine remaining ingredients. Pour over cabbage.
2. Cook, covered, for 9 to 11 minutes, or until cabbage is tender. Stir once during cooking period.

Stuffed Eggplant

4 servings

2 medium eggplants
2 medium onions, chopped
1 pound ground lamb
1 beef bouillon cube
1 can (8 ounces) tomato sauce

½ teaspoon oregano
2 tablespoons chopped parsley
½ teaspoon salt
¼ teaspoon pepper
½ cup dry bread crumbs

1. Wash eggplant and cut in half lengthwise. Scoop out insides, leaving a shell 1 inch thick. Chop eggplant pulp in medium chunks. Set aside.
2. Put onion in a 1½-quart casserole. Crumble in lamb. Cook, covered, for about 6 minutes, or just until lamb loses its pink color. Drain off fat.
3. Dissolve bouillon cube in ½ cup hot water. Stir into cooked lamb with 3 tablespoons tomato sauce and the chopped eggplant pulp.
4. Cook, covered, for 7 to 8 minutes, stirring occasionally.
5. Remove from oven; stir in oregano, parsley, salt, and pepper. Fill eggplant halves with mixture. Sprinkle bread crumbs over top. Streak remaining tomato sauce over top of crumbs.
6. Place eggplant halves in a glass baking dish. Cook, covered, for about 18 to 20 minutes, or just until eggplant is tender.

Stuffed Green Peppers

4 to 6 servings

4 large green peppers
1 pound ground beef
1 medium onion, finely chopped
1 teaspoon salt

¼ teaspoon pepper
1½ cups cooked rice
1 can (16 ounces) tomato sauce

1. Wash peppers. Cut in half lengthwise and remove seeds and white membrane.
2. Crumble beef in a 1½-quart glass casserole. Add onion. Cook, uncovered, for 7 to 8 minutes, stirring once during cooking period to break up meat. Cook until meat loses its red color.
3. Stir in salt, pepper, rice, and half of the tomato sauce. Fill green pepper halves with mixture, mounding mixture on top. Place in a glass baking dish. Top each pepper with a dribble of remaining tomato sauce.
4. Cook, covered, for 15 to 17 minutes, or just until peppers are tender.

Cooked Rice

6 to 8 servings

2 cups long-grained rice   **1 teaspoon salt**

1. Combine rice, salt, and 2 cups boiling water in a 1½- to 2-quart casserole.
2. Cook, covered, for about 23 minutes, or until almost tender.
3. Let stand, covered, 6 minutes. Fluff with a fork before serving.

Eggs in Nests

8 servings

8 small, firm-ripe tomatoes   **1 large onion, chopped**
¼ cup chopped parsley   **8 eggs**
¼ cup butter or margarine   **Salt and pepper to taste**

1. Cut tops from tomatoes. Scoop out pulp and turn shells upside down on paper towels to drain. Discard seeds, chop pulp, and mix with parsley.
2. Combine butter and onion in a small mixing bowl. Cook, covered, for about 6 minutes. Add parsley-tomato pulp mixture.
3. Stir mixture well and divide into tomato shells. Break 1 egg into each tomato shell. Season lightly with salt and pepper.
4. Place tomatoes in a baking dish. Cook, covered, for about 1 minute, or until eggs are set to desired degree of doneness.

Frozen Carrots

3 to 4 servings

Place 1 10-ounce package frozen carrots in a 1-quart casserole, icy side up. Cook, covered, for 9 to 10 minutes, stirring once during cooking time.

Carrots

3 to 4 servings

Wash carrots well. Very tiny fresh spring carrots may be left whole. Mature carrots should be scraped or peeled. Cut carrots into thin rounds or slivers.

Prepare 6 medium carrots. Place in a 1- or 1½-quart casserole. Add 2 tablespoons water. Cook, covered, for 10 to 11 minutes, stirring once during cooking period. Drain, season to taste, and serve.

Cranberry Carrots

4 servings

6 to 8 carrots   **¼ cup jellied cranberry sauce**
¼ cup butter or margarine   **Salt and pepper to taste**

1. Cook carrots according to directions. Add about 1 minute to cooking time for the larger number of carrots.
2. Place butter in a 1½- to 2-quart casserole. Cook for about 2 to 2½ minutes, or until butter is melted.
3. Add cranberry sauce. Cook, for about 2 minutes, stirring once or twice, until cranberry sauce is melted.
4. Add cooked carrots and toss gently. Season to taste with salt and pepper.

Tangy Glazed Carrots
3 to 4 servings

6 carrots
⅓ cup orange juice
2 tablespoons sugar
¼ teaspoon ground cloves

¼ teaspoon salt
½ jar (5 ounces) pineapple cheese
spread

1. Peel carrots. Slice into rings. Cook according to directions.
2. Combine juice, sugar, cloves, salt, and cheese spread. Blend thoroughly. Pour mixture over hot cooked carrots.
3. Cook, uncovered, for about 2½ minutes, until cheese melts and mixture is piping hot.

Cauliflower
3 to 4 servings

Remove outer leaves and stalks from 1 medium head of cauliflower. Separate into flowerets. Place in a 1½-quart casserole. Add 2 to 3 tablespoons water. Cook for 11 to 12 minutes, or until cauliflower is tender. Stir once during cooking period.

Frozen Cauliflower
3 to 4 servings

Place 1 package (10 ounces) frozen cauliflower in a 1-quart saucepan, icy side up. Cook, covered, for 11 to 12 minutes, stirring once during cooking period.

Cheesed Cauliflower
4 servings

1 medium head cauliflower
3 tablespoons olive oil
1 large onion, thinly sliced
¼ teaspoon salt

Dash of pepper
¼ cup fine dry bread crumbs
¼ cup grated Cheddar cheese

1. Remove outer leaves and stalks from cauliflower. Separate into flowerets. Cook according to preceding directions.
2. Put olive oil in a 1-quart casserole. Add onion. Cook, uncovered, for about 6 minutes, or until onions are limp and tender. Stir once or twice during cooking period.
3. Add salt, pepper, and bread crumbs.
4. Drain cauliflower and leave in original casserole. Top with hot onion mixture. Sprinkle cheese over top.
5. Cook, uncovered, for 3 to 4 minutes, or until cheese is melted and cauliflower is piping hot.

Cauliflower and Tomatoes

4 servings

1 medium head cauliflower
1 clove garlic
3 tablespoons olive oil

½ teaspoon salt
½ cup cooked tomatoes
2 tablespoons grated Parmesan cheese

1. Remove outer leaves and stalks from cauliflower. Separate into flowerets. Cook according to directions but undercook just slightly.
2. Combine garlic and olive oil in a 1½-quart casserole. Cook, uncovered, for 2 minutes.
3. Remove garlic. Add hot drained cauliflower to oil.
4. Cook, uncovered, for 4 minutes.
5. Add salt and tomatoes. Cook, covered, for about 6 minutes, or until piping hot. Stir once or twice during cooking time.
6. Sprinkle top with cheese and serve immediately.

Celery

3 servings

Remove leaves and trim roots from a bunch of celery. Separate into stalks and wash thoroughly. Scrape off any discoloration with a knife. Use outer branches for cooking. Reserve inner branches to serve raw.

Slice stalks crosswise into half moons, about 1½-inches thick. Use 6 stalks, making about 4 cups of slices. Place in a 1½-quart casserole. Add 3 to 4 tablespoons water. Cook, covered, for 10 to 12 minutes, or just until crisply tender. Stir once during cooking period. Drain and season to taste.

Sweet and Sour Celery

3 to 4 servings

2 cups thinly sliced celery
1 bay leaf
3 whole cloves
2 tablespoons sugar

3 tablespoons vinegar
2 tablespoons butter or margarine
Salt and pepper to taste

1. Place celery, bay leaf, cloves, and ¼ cup water in a 1½-quart casserole.
2. Cook, covered, for 10 to 12 minutes, or just until celery is crisply tender.
3. Add sugar, vinegar, and butter. Toss lightly. Cook, covered, for 2 minutes, or until butter is melted and celery is piping hot. Season to taste.

Corn on the Cob

Corn should be selected with fresh green, not dried-out, husks. Just before cooking, remove husks, all silk, and any blemishes or discolorations.

Wrap each ear of corn in a piece of waxed paper and twist ends tightly together. Place in oven, with about 1 inch space between. Cook no more than 4 ears of fresh corn at a time, for 15 to 17 minutes, or until tender.

For frozen corn, wrap each ear in a piece of waxed paper and twist ends together. Place no more than 4 at a time in the oven, separated from each other by about 1 inch of space. Cook for 20 to 22 minutes.

Frozen Cut Corn

Place 1 package (10 ounces) frozen kernel corn in a 1-quart casserole. Cook, covered, for 8 to 9 minutes, stirring once during cooking period.

Corn Pudding   4 servings

2 tablespoons butter or margarine

2 tablespoons all-purpose flour

1 can (1 pound) whole kernel corn, drained

2 cups milk

2 eggs, well beaten

1 teaspoon salt

½ teaspoon pepper

1. Melt butter in a 1½-quart glass casserole for 2 minutes.
2. Stir in flour to make a smooth paste. Add remaining ingredients and blend well.
3. Cook, covered, for 12 to 14 minutes, stirring twice.
4. Let stand, loosely covered, 2 minutes before serving.

Note: Good with ham or pork chops for a hearty winter dinner.

Erik's Eggplant   6 servings

4 slices bacon

1 medium onion, chopped

1 medium green pepper, seeded and chopped

1 1-pound eggplant

2 teaspoons salt

¼ teaspoon pepper

1 can (8 ounces) tomato sauce

½ cup grated Parmesan cheese

1. Place bacon on inverted saucer in an oblong glass baking dish. Cover with waxed paper. Cook for about 6 minutes, or until bacon is crisp. Reserve bacon and drippings.
2. Put onion and pepper in a 1½-quart casserole. Pour bacon fat over top of onion.
3. Cook, covered, for about 4 minutes.
4. Peel eggplant and cut in cubes. Add to onion mixture in casserole with salt, pepper, tomato sauce, and 1 cup water.
5. Cook, covered, for 8 to 10 minutes.
6. Remove from oven and sprinkle cheese over top of mixture. Crumble bacon and sprinkle over top of cheese.
7. Cook, covered, for 10 to 12 minutes.
8. Let stand about 4 minutes before serving.

Sautéed Mushrooms   2 to 4 servings

½ pound fresh mushrooms

1 clove garlic, minced

⅓ cup butter or margarine

1. Clean mushrooms and slice. Put in an 8-inch round dish or a skillet. Add garlic and butter.

2. Cook, covered, for 6 to 7 minutes.
3. Serve with roast beef or steak, or on crisp toast as a main dish.

Peas
4 servings

Shell 2 pounds fresh peas and place in a 1½-quart casserole. Add 2 to 3 tablespoons water. Cook, covered, for 10 to 11 minutes, stirring once during cooking time. Season to taste and serve.

Frozen Peas
3 to 4 servings

Place 1 package (10 ounces) peas in a 1-quart casserole, icy side up. Cook, covered, for 7 to 8 minutes, stirring once during cooking time.

Baked Potatoes

Select baking potatoes of uniform size if possible so that they will all be cooked at the same time. Scrub potatoes with a stiff brush. Remove any bad spots with a sharp knife. Cut a thin slice from one end of each potato. Prick entire surface of potato with the tines of a fork.

Place potatoes on paper plates in the oven with at least 1 inch of space between them. Cook given amount of time. It is easy to test potatoes with a fork or skewer to determine when they are done, so try shorter cooking time first and then increase time as needed:

2 small, 8 to 10 minutes; 4 small, 10 to 11 minutes;
6 small, 16 to 17 minutes; 1 medium, 10 to 11 minutes;
2 medium, 10 to 11 minutes; 4 medium, 23 to 25 minutes.

Boiled Potatoes
4 servings

Potatoes should be cut in quarters if they are small, in eighths if they are larger. The pieces should all be about the same size for uniform cooking. Peel 4 medium potatoes and cut up. Place in a 1½-quart casserole. Cover with water and add ½ teaspoon salt. Cook, covered, for 22 to 25 minutes, or until potatoes are tender.

Hashed Potatoes
4 servings

⅓ cup butter or margarine
½ cup coarsely chopped onions

4 baked potatoes, cold
Salt and pepper to taste

1. In a 1½-quart casserole put butter and onion. Cook, uncovered, for 9 to 10 minutes, stirring occasionally.
2. Peel potatoes and cut in small chunks. Stir into onion in casserole. Season to taste. Cook, uncovered, for 9 to 10 minutes, stirring occasionally.

Scalloped Potatoes

6 to 8 servings

5 cups (about 6 medium) peeled and
   thinly sliced raw potatoes
3 onions, sliced
Salt and pepper to taste
3 teaspoons dry mustard, divided
3 tablespoons grated Parmesan cheese,
   divided

3 tablespoons all-purpose flour, divided
3 tablespoons butter or margarine
3 cups milk
Paprika

1. Line bottom of a 3-quart casserole with one-third of the potatoes and cover with one-third of the onion. Add salt and pepper to taste, sprinkle on 1 teaspoon mustard, 1 tablespoon cheese, and 1 tablespoon flour. Repeat process twice with remaining potatoes, onion, seasonings, cheese, and flour. Dot with butter. Pour milk over top. Sprinkle with paprika.
2. Cook, covered, for 50 minutes, rotating casserole several times.
3. Remove from oven and let stand at least 5 minutes before serving.

Sweet Potatoes

4 servings

Select sweet potatoes of approximately the same size for uniform cooking. Scrub 4 medium sweet potatoes. Remove any spots or blemishes with a sharp knife. Prick entire surface of each potato with a fork. Place at least 1 inch apart on paper plates in oven. Cook for 12 to 15 minutes, or until tender.

Candied Sweet Potatoes

6 servings

6 medium sweet potatoes
1 cup brown sugar, firmly packed

2 tablespoons butter or margarine

1. Cook sweet potatoes according to preceding directions. Peel and slice. Arrange in a 2-quart casserole.
2. Combine remaining ingredients with ⅓ cup water in a 2-cup measure. Cook, uncovered, for 5 to 6 minutes, or until mixture comes to a boil.
3. Pour over top of potatoes. Cook, covered, for 12 to 13 minutes, or until heated through, spooning glaze over potatoes occasionally.

White Sauce

1 cup

2 tablespoons butter or margarine
2 tablespoons flour
½ teaspoon salt

Dash of pepper
1 cup milk

1. In a 2-cup measure melt butter for 30 seconds.
2. Stir in flour, salt, and pepper. Cook for 1 minute.
3. Gradually stir in milk. Cook, uncovered, for 4 to 4½ minutes, stirring occasionally during last half of cooking time. Remove and stir briskly.

Variations: For a thick white sauce use 3 tablespoons butter and 3 tablespoons flour with 1 cup milk. For a thin white sauce use 1 tablespoon butter and 1 tablespoon flour.

108

Sandwiches

Hot dogs are a kid's best friend. In the microwave oven they cook so fast that even the kids can't complain about starving while waiting for lunch to be ready. The franks can be cooked alone or popped into a bun, and the whole thing done in no time. Open-faced or closed, meat or fish, to be eaten from a plate or in the hand—delicious sandwiches of all kinds are prepared as if by magic in the microwave oven.

Brapples

2 to 3 medium apples
¼ teaspoon lemon juice
¾ cup brown sugar

½ cup chopped walnuts
4 slices white bread, buttered
4 slices process American cheese

1. Peel, core, and slice apples in very thin slices.
2. Mix with lemon juice, brown sugar, and walnuts.
3. Divide over bread slices. Top with cheese.
4. Place in a 9-inch square dish.
5. Cook for 3½ minutes, or until apples are tender.

Variation: Turn these into a last-minute dessert by topping each with a table-spoon of sour cream and a sprinkling of brown sugar and nuts.

Bermuda Grill

6 servings

2 cups chopped Bermuda onions
1 teaspoon salt
¼ teaspoon white pepper

½ cup Sauterne
12 slices Swiss cheese
12 slices rye bread, toasted

1. Place chopped onion in a shallow dish; sprinkle with salt and pepper. Add Sauterne.
2. Cover and let stand at least 1 hour, stirring every 15 minutes; drain.
3. Place a slice of cheese on each of 6 toast slices.
4. Divide marinated onion over sandwiches and top with another slice of cheese, then a second slice of bread.
5. Place each sandwich on a paper plate. Cook one at a time, for 2 to 2½ minutes, or until cheese is melted.

Hot Salad Cheesewiches

4 servings

1 cup shredded Cheddar cheese
½ cup diced cucumber
1 tablespoon minced onion
¼ cup dairy sour cream
⅛ teaspoon pepper

⅛ teaspoon chili powder
4 slices bread
4 large thick tomato slices
8 slices dill pickle
Paprika

1. Combine cheese, cucumber, onion, sour cream, and seasonings.
2. Toast bread lightly. Place each slice of bread on a paper plate.
3. Arrange a tomato slice and 2 pickle slices on each slice of bread.
4. Divide the cheese mixture over the 4 slices, and sprinkle with paprika.
5. Cook each sandwich separately, for 2 to 2½ minutes, or until cheese melts and mixture is thoroughly heated.

Geri's Baked Brunchwiches

6 servings

12 to 14 slices white bread
Butter or margarine
½ pound grated Cheddar cheese
1 teaspoon dry mustard

6 eggs
2 cups milk
½ teaspoon salt
Paprika

1. Remove crust from bread slices. Butter each slice and cut in quarters or small chunks. Put a layer of bread in a 2- to 3-quart casserole. Sprinkle half the cheese over bread. Sprinkle half the mustard over cheese. Repeat layers with bread, cheese, and mustard.
2. Beat eggs with milk and salt. Pour over top of bread and cheese layers. Sprinkle generously with paprika.
3. Cover with foil or casserole lid and refrigerate overnight.
4. Before cooking, cut 2-inch strips of aluminum foil. Place over ends of dish. Cook for 15 minutes, rotating casserole after 8 minutes.
5. Remove from oven and remove aluminum foil. Cook for 13 to 15 minutes, rotating casserole after 8 minutes.
6. Remove from oven, cover with foil or casserole lid, and let stand 3 to 4 minutes before serving.

Cheese Roll-Ups

6 servings

4 slices bacon
1 loaf (1 pound) unsliced white bread
1 cup grated process American cheese
¼ cup chopped stuffed olives

¼ teaspoon Worcestershire sauce
1 can (10½ ounces) condensed cream of mushroom soup, undiluted
¼ cup milk

1. Cook bacon according to directions on page 60 and reserve.
2. Cut crusts from loaf and cut loaf into 6 horizontal slices.
3. Crumble bacon and combine with cheese, olives, Worcestershire, and ⅓ cup of the mushroom soup.
4. Spread 3 tablespoons of the mixture on each slice of bread. Roll up, jelly-roll fashion.
5. Place each roll-up on a paper plate. Cook one at a time, for 3½ to 4 minutes, or until heated through.
6. Combine remaining mushroom soup and milk in a 2-cup glass measuring cup. Cook for 4 to 4½ minutes.
7. Serve mushroom sauce over roll-ups.

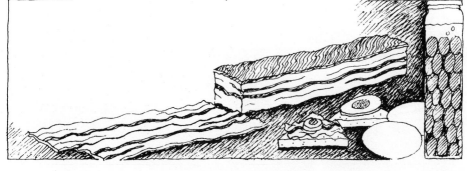

FOLLOWING PAGES: Left, *Reuben Sandwich, page 115;* right, *Hot Dogs and Sausage and Pepper Hero, page 116.*

Ranchburgers

6 servings

6 slices bacon
1½ cups grated process American
  cheese
2 tablespoons finely chopped onion

¼ cup catsup
1 tablespoon prepared mustard
6 sandwich buns, split

1. Cook bacon according to directions on p. 60. Crumble bacon and combine with remaining ingredients except buns.
2. Spread 3 tablespoons cheese mixture on bottom half of each bun and cover with bun top.
3. Wrap each sandwich in waxed paper and twist ends of paper.
4. Cook each sandwich separately, for 2½ to 3 minutes, or until heated through.

Second-Act Ham

3 to 4 servings

¾ cup hollandaise sauce
4 slices bread, toasted
Ham slices from leftover baked ham

1 can (8 ounces) asparagus, drained,
  or 9 to 12 fresh asparagus, cooked
2 hard-cooked eggs, sliced (optional)

1. Prepare hollandaise sauce, using your favorite recipe. Cover with waxed paper and set aside.
2. Arrange toast, cut in quarters, in individual casseroles. Put desired amount of ham on top of toast. Arrange 3 or 4 asparagus spears on top of ham. Add ½ egg, sliced, on top if desired.
3. Cook, covered with waxed paper, 1 casserole at a time, for about 2 minutes, or until heated.
4. Top with hollandaise sauce. Cover with waxed paper and heat for 1 minute. If hollandaise sauce is cold, double the heating time.

Sardine Buns

6 servings

¼ pound process American cheese,
  cubed
5 hard-cooked eggs, chopped
½ cup drained mashed sardines
1 tablespoon minced green pepper

2 tablespoons minced onion
3 tablespoons chopped stuffed olives
2 tablespoons pickle relish, drained
½ cup mayonnaise
6 hamburger buns, split and buttered

1. Combine all ingredients except buns.
2. Fill each bun with cheese mixture.
3. Wrap each sandwich in waxed paper and twist ends of paper.
4. Cook one at a time, for 2 to 2½ minutes, or until rolls are hot.

Note: These may be prepared in advance and refrigerated in their waxed paper wrapping. Cook before serving.

Hot Swiss Tuna

4 servings

4 hamburger buns
1 can (6½ or 7 ounces) tuna fish, drained and flaked
½ cup finely shredded Swiss cheese
1 cup chopped celery

¼ cup mayonnaise
2 tablespoons catsup
1 teaspoon lemon juice
Salt and pepper to taste

1. Split hamburger buns.
2. Combine tuna, cheese, celery, mayonnaise, catsup, and lemon juice. Season to taste with salt and pepper.
3. Divide tuna mixture among four buns.
4. Wrap each sandwich in waxed paper and twist ends of paper.
5. Cook one at a time, for 2 to 2½ minutes, or until rolls are hot.

Barbecued Beef Strips on Buns

6 servings

½ cup butter or margarine
1 pound top round steak, cut into thin strips
1 teaspoon salt
⅛ teaspoon garlic salt
⅛ teaspoon pepper
1 can (10½ ounces) beef broth

1 can (8 ounces) tomato paste
2 tablespoons cornstarch
1 teaspoon sugar
1 can (4 ounces) sliced mushrooms, drained
¼ cup dry red wine
6 buns

1. Put butter in a 2- or 3-quart casserole. Cook, uncovered, in oven for 30 seconds, or just until butter melts.
2. Put strips of meat in casserole and toss lightly so that meat is coated with butter. Add salt, garlic salt, and pepper.
3. Cook, uncovered, for 9 to 10 minutes, stirring occasionally.
4. Add beef broth and tomato paste. Combine cornstarch and sugar and stir into mixture.
5. Cook, covered, for 6 minutes, stirring at least once during cooking period.
6. Add mushrooms and wine. Cook, covered, for about 3 minutes, or until mushrooms are hot.
7. Let stand, covered, 4 to 5 minutes before serving.
8. Serve beef strips, with sauce, in heated buns.

Reuben Sandwich

4 servings

8 slices dark rye or pumpernickel bread
Butter or margarine
½ pound thinly sliced corned beef

1 can (8 ounces) sauerkraut, drained
Thousand Island dressing
4 slices Swiss cheese

1. Toast bread. Butter lightly.
2. Arrange sliced corned beef on 4 slices of toast. Divide sauerkraut among sandwiches. Top with Thousand Island dressing. Top each with a slice of Swiss cheese. Top with other slices of toast, buttered side down.
3. Place each sandwich on a paper plate.
4. Cook one at a time, for 1½ to 2 minutes, or just until cheese is melted.

Sausage and Pepper Hero

4 servings

4 Italian sausages

½ cup prepared barbecue sauce

1 green pepper, seeded and cut in
strips

4 hero rolls

1. Place a layer of paper towels in an 8-inch square dish. Place sausage on towels. Cover with paper towels.
2. Cook for 12 minutes, turning midway in cooking period. Drain off fat and reserve.
3. Cook barbecue sauce with pepper strips in a 2-cup glass measure for 2 to 3 minutes.
4. Split hero rolls almost in half. Place 1 cooked sausage in each roll. Top with one-quarter of the sauce and peppers. Wrap each roll in waxed paper and twist ends of paper.
5. Cook, one at a time, for 2 to 2½ minutes, or until rolls are piping hot.

Hot Dogs

1 serving

1 frankfurter roll

Prepared mustard

Pickle relish

1 frankfurter

1. Spread roll with mustard and relish. Place hot dog in roll. Wrap in waxed paper and twist ends securely.
2. Cook for 1½ to 2 minutes. To cook 2 at a time or 3 at a time, follow given amounts of time: for 2 hot dogs, 3 to 3½ minutes; for 3 hot dogs, 4 to 4½ minutes.

Beans and Things in Buns

4 servings

6 slices bacon, cut in pieces

1 medium onion, chopped

4 frankfurters, cut in small pieces

1 teaspoon prepared mustard

1 teaspoon catsup

1 can (1 pound) pork and beans in
tomato sauce

4 frankfurter buns

1. Put bacon pieces in 1½-quart casserole.
2. Cook, covered, for 4 minutes. Stir.
3. Add chopped onion.
4. Cook, covered, for 2 minutes. Stir well.
5. Add frankfurters. Cook, covered, for 5 minutes, stirring once. Add mustard, catsup, and beans and mix well.
6. Cook, covered, for 6 to 7 minutes, or until hot, stirring once during cooking period. Serve hot in heated buns.

116

OPPOSITE: *Cheeseburger, page 120.*

Asparagus Egg Specials

6 servings

6 slices white bread
2 tablespoons soft butter or margarine
3 hard-cooked eggs, sliced
24 cooked green asparagus spears
   (see page 94)

Salt and pepper to taste
1 can (8 ounces) tomato sauce
¼ teaspoon sugar
½ teaspoon oregano
2 tablespoons slivered almonds

1. Toast bread and spread lightly with butter.
2. Arrange egg slices on toast and top each toast slice with 4 asparagus spears. Sprinkle with salt and pepper.
3. Combine tomato sauce, sugar, and oregano.
4. Place toast slices in a 9-inch square dish. Pour tomato sauce over and sprinkle with nuts.
5. Cook for 3 to 5 minutes, or until heated through.

Chicken Crumpets

8 servings

4 tablespoons butter or margarine
¼ cup all-purpose flour
1 teaspoon salt
⅛ teaspoon pepper
2 cups milk

3 tablespoons sherry
2 cups diced cooked chicken
Paprika
4 crumpets
8 baked ham slices

1. Place butter in a 1-quart casserole. Cook for 30 seconds, or until butter is melted.
2. Stir in flour, salt, and pepper. Cook for 1 minute.
3. Stir in milk. Cook for 5 to 6 minutes, stirring at 2 minutes and again at 4 minutes, or until mixture is thickened.
4. Remove from oven and stir in sherry, chicken, and a dash of paprika.
5. Split, toast, and butter crumpets. Place each crumpet on a paper plate.
6. Place 1 slice of ham on each crumpet half. Divide chicken mixture over ham slices and sprinkle lightly with paprika.
7. Cook 4 at a time, for 3 to 4 minutes, or until heated through.

Chicken Tacos

10 to 12 servings

½ cup chopped onions
2 tablespoons butter or margarine
2 cups coarsely diced cooked chicken
1 can (7½ ounces) taco sauce
¼ teaspoon salt

¼ teaspoon garlic salt
10 to 12 fully cooked taco shells
Grated Cheddar cheese
Shredded lettuce
Chopped fresh tomatoes

1. Cook onion and butter in a 1-quart casserole for 3 to 4 minutes.
2. Add chicken, taco sauce, salt, and garlic salt. Cover with a paper towel.
3. Cook for 8 to 9 minutes, or until mixture thickens and is hot.
4. Spoon filling into taco shells. Place tacos in a straight-sided glass dish so that they will stand upright.

5. Cook, covered with waxed paper, for 3 to 4 minutes, or until tacos are piping hot.
6. Serve with cheese, lettuce, and tomato in side dishes to sprinkle as desired over top of hot filling.

Turkey Glory
6 servings

6 slices cooked turkey
6 slices white bread, toasted and buttered
1 cup milk
1 package (8 ounces) cream cheese, at room temperature
½ cup grated Parmesan cheese
¼ teaspoon garlic salt
½ cup sliced stuffed olives
Paprika

1. Place turkey on toast.
2. In a 1-quart ovenproof casserole, gradually add milk to cream cheese, mixing until well blended.
3. Cook for 3 minutes.
4. Stir. Cook again for 2 minutes.
5. Remove from oven and stir in Parmesan cheese, garlic salt, and olives.
6. Cover each sandwich with sauce; sprinkle with paprika.

Sloppy Joe Sandwich
6 servings

1 pound ground beef
½ cup chopped onions
½ cup chopped green pepper
½ teaspoon paprika
1 can (8 ounces) tomato sauce
1 teaspoon salt
Pinch of sugar
Freshly ground pepper to taste
Toasted hamburger buns

1. Crumble beef in a 2-quart casserole. Add onion, pepper, and paprika.
2. Cook, uncovered, for 7 to 8 minutes, or until meat loses its red color. Stir once during cooking time.
3. Break up meat with a fork. Add remaining ingredients except buns and blend well.
4. Cook, covered, for 15 to 17 minutes, stirring occasionally.
5. Spoon onto bottom half of toasted hamburger buns; cover with top half.

Note: The Sloppy Joe mixture can be made up well in advance and kept in the refrigerator. To serve, remove any congealed fat on top of mixture. Spoon desired amount of meat on hamburger buns or hard rolls, spreading mixture out to edges. Place single serving on a small plate. Heat for 2 to 3 minutes, until mixture is piping hot.

119

Witches' Brew Heroes

6 servings

1 medium onion, chopped
1 small green pepper, seeded and
   chopped
1 clove garlic, peeled and halved
1 pound ground beef, crumbled
1 can (1 pound) whole tomatoes

½ teaspoon chili powder
¼ teaspoon salt
¼ teaspoon sugar
¼ teaspoon hot-pepper sauce
⅛ teaspoon ground cumin
6 hero rolls

1. Combine onion, green pepper, garlic, and beef in 2-quart casserole.
2. Cook, uncovered, for 7 to 8 minutes, or until meat loses its red color. Stir once to break up meat.
3. Break up large meat chunks with a fork. Mash tomatoes with a fork so that tomatoes are in small chunks. Add to meat mixture with chili powder, salt, sugar, hot-pepper sauce, and cumin.
4. Cook, covered, for 15 to 17 minutes, stirring occasionally.
5. Remove garlic. Serve on hero rolls.

Paul Bunyans

6 servings

1 pound ground beef
½ cup finely chopped onion
½ cup finely chopped green pepper
½ cup chopped pitted ripe olives
1 can (6 ounces) tomato paste
1 teaspoon salt

Freshly ground pepper to taste
½ teaspoon poultry seasoning
½ teaspoon hot-pepper sauce
½ teaspoon chili powder
1 teaspoon Worcestershire sauce
Toasted hamburger buns

1. Crumble beef into a 2-quart casserole. Add onion and green pepper.
2. Cook, uncovered, for 7 to 8 minutes, or until meat has lost its red color. Stir once during cooking time.
3. Break up meat chunks with a fork. Add olives, tomato paste, salt, pepper, poultry seasoning, hot-pepper sauce, chili powder, and Worcestershire. Stir well. Add 1 to 2 tablespoons of water if mixture is dry.
4. Cook, covered, for 15 to 17 minutes, stirring occasionally.
5. Serve immediately on toasted buns.

Cheeseburgers

4 servings

1 pound ground beef
Salt and pepper

4 hamburger buns, toasted
4 slices process American cheese

1. Season ground beef to taste with salt and pepper. Shape into 4 patties. Place in an 8-inch square baking dish.
2. Cook, covered with waxed paper, for 3 minutes.
3. Turn patties over. Cook, covered, for 3 minutes, or to the desired degree of doneness.
4. Place 1 patty on each hamburger bun. Top with a slice of cheese. Place each bun on a small paper plate.
5. Cook 1 or 2 at a time, for 1½ minutes, or until cheese melts.

Open-Face Hamburgers

6 servings

1 pound ground beef
1 teaspoon salt
1 teaspoon oregano
½ teaspoon dry mustard
Freshly ground pepper to taste
1 tablespoon instant minced onion

½ cup tomato juice
1 cup shredded Cheddar cheese
3 hamburger buns, halved and toasted
6 slices tomato
2 tablespoons butter or margarine

1. Crumble ground beef into a 1½-quart casserole or an 8-inch round glass cake dish.
2. Cook, uncovered, for 7 to 8 minutes, or until meat has lost its red color. Stir once during cooking time.
3. Break up meat with a fork. Add salt, oregano, dry mustard, pepper, onion, tomato juice, and cheese. Stir thoroughly.
4. Cook, covered, for 2 to 3 minutes, or until cheese is melted and mixture is piping hot.
5. Place toasted hamburger halves on a broiler pan. Spoon hamburger mixture on top of each bun. Top each with a slice of tomato. Dot with butter. Place under broiler on conventional range and broil until tomatoes are lightly browned.

Old Mystic

6 servings

1 can (7½ ounces) crab meat, drained
1 can (5 ounces) shrimp, drained
2 packages (3 ounces each) cream cheese, at room temperature
½ cup chopped almonds
2 tablespoons dry white wine
2 teaspoons lemon juice
1 teaspoon minced onion

1 teaspoon prepared horseradish
1 teaspoon prepared mustard
½ teaspoon salt
¼ teaspoon white pepper
⅛ teaspoon cayenne
6 French rolls
⅓ cup shredded Gruyere cheese

1. Pick over crab meat and remove any bits of shells or cartilege. Combine with shrimp and cream cheese and blend well. Add almonds, white wine, lemon juice, onion, horseradish, mustard, salt, pepper, and cayenne.
2. Remove top third from each roll and scoop out inside, being careful not to puncture shell. Spoon mixture evenly into 6 shells. Sprinkle cheese over top of filling. Place tops on rolls.
3. Place 2 rolls at a time on paper towels or paper plates in oven. Cook for 2 to 3 minutes, or until filling is piping hot and cheese has melted.

121

Turkey Gobble-Up

6 servings

6 English muffins
Butter
6 slices bacon
1 large avocado
¼ cup mayonnaise
¼ cup dairy sour cream
1 tablespoon lemon juice

Dash of hot-pepper sauce
12 slices (1 ounce each) cooked turkey
breast
12 slices tomato
1 jar (8 ounces) pasteurized process
cheese spread

1. Split, toast, and butter English muffins.
2. Cut bacon strips into 4 pieces each. Place on a paper towel in an oblong baking dish. Cover with a paper towel and cook for 3½ minutes.
3. Peel, seed, and mash avocado. Combine with mayonnaise, sour cream, lemon juice, and hot-pepper sauce.
4. Spread avocado mixture generously on each muffin half. Arrange 1 slice each of turkey and tomato on each muffin half. Spread 1 tablespoon cheese on each tomato. Top each with 2 pieces of cooked bacon.
5. Place 6 halves in an oblong baking dish. Cook for 2 to 2½ minutes, or until cheese is hot and bubbly.

Ham and Asparagus Cheese Sandwiches

4 servings

4 slices bread, toasted
4 slices thinly sliced ham

8 slices Swiss cheese
1 can (15 ounces) asparagus spears

1. Place toasted bread in a baking dish.
2. Cover each slice with 1 slice ham, 1 slice cheese, and 5 asparagus spears. Top with second slice of cheese.
3. Cook for 10 minutes.
4. Garnish with paprika if desired.

Beverages

Single servings of coffee or cocoa, made in mugs or paper cups, are heated in seconds and are certainly a boon for the busy homemaker. If beverages cool off, the microwave oven will bring them back to serving temperature in a flash. Don't forget that milk boils over easily and rapidly —so when making beverages with milk, do not fill the container, large or small, to the brim.

Mulled Wine

8 to 10 servings

1 cup sugar
2 pieces (1 inch each) stick cinnamon
1 lemon, sliced

24 whole cloves
4 cups orange juice
1 quart Burgundy wine

1. Combine sugar, cinnamon, lemon, and cloves with ½ cup water in a 3-quart casserole.
2. Heat for 4 minutes.
3. Add orange juice and Burgundy.
4. Heat for 7 minutes.
5. Garnish with lemon or pineapple slices, if desired.

Hot Toddy

1 serving

1 teaspoon sugar
1 piece (1 inch) stick cinnamon

1 slice lemon, studded with 2 cloves
2 ounces bourbon

1. Combine sugar, cinnamon, and lemon slice with ½ cup water in a 1-cup measuring cup.
2. Cook for 7 to 8 minutes.
3. Meantime, place bourbon in a serving cup or mug.
4. Remove hot mixture from oven and pour over bourbon. Stir and serve.

Mulled Pineapple Juice

10 servings

1 can (46 ounces) pineapple juice
1 piece (2 inches) stick cinnamon
⅛ teaspoon ground nutmeg

⅛ teaspoon ground allspice
Dash ground cloves

1. Combine all ingredients in a 2-quart casserole.
2. Heat for 7 to 8 minutes.

Spicy Apple Nog

5 to 6 servings

2 eggs, separated
¼ cup sugar
½ teaspoon salt
½ teaspoon ground cinnamon

Dash of ground nutmeg
⅔ cup apple juice
3 cups milk
½ cup heavy cream, whipped

1. Place egg yolks in a 2-quart casserole. Beat lightly with a fork.
2. Stir in sugar, salt, cinnamon, nutmeg, and apple juice until well blended. Stir in milk.
3. Cook for 7 to 8 minutes.
4. Meantime, beat egg whites in a 2-quart mixing bowl.
5. Remove milk mixture from oven and pour quickly over egg whites, stirring rapidly.
6. Top each serving with a mound of whipped cream.

OPPOSITE: *Hot Instant Tea, page 128; Instant Coffee, page 127; Instant Cocoa, Mulled Cider, Hot Spiced Cranberry Punch, page 126.*

Hot Spiced Cranberry Punch

6 servings

1½ cups cranberry juice cocktail
4 whole cloves
1 piece (2 inches) stick cinnamon
3 tablespoons sugar

1 can (6 ounces) frozen lemonade
   concentrate, thawed
3 orange slices, cut in half
6 maraschino cherries

1. Combine cranberry juice, cloves, and cinnamon stick with 1½ cups water in 1-quart measuring cup.
2. Cook for 10 minutes.
3. Cover and let stand 1 minute.
4. Remove spices.
5. Stir in sugar until dissolved.
6. Blend in lemonade.
7. Cook for 4 to 5 minutes.
8. Serve hot, garnished with half an orange slice and a maraschino cherry on a toothpick.

Mulled Cider

4 servings

3 cups apple cider
3 tablespoons brown sugar
⅛ teaspoon salt
Dash of ground nutmeg

½ teaspoon whole allspice
½ teaspoon whole cloves
1 stick cinnamon
2 orange slices, cut in half

1. Place apple cider, brown sugar, salt, and nutmeg in 1-quart measuring cup.
2. Tie allspice, cloves, and cinnamon in cheesecloth and drop into cider.
3. Cook for 7 to 8 minutes. Let stand 5 minutes.
4. Remove spice bag and serve hot, garnished with orange slices.

Mexican Chocolate

4 servings

½ cup semisweet chocolate bits
1 tablespoon instant coffee
½ teaspoon vanilla extract

¼ teaspoon ground cinnamon
2 cups milk

1. Place chocolate, coffee, and ½ cup water in a 4-cup measuring cup.
2. Heat for 5 minutes.
3. Remove from oven and stir in remaining ingredients.
4. Heat for 8 minutes.

Instant Cocoa

1 serving

¾ cup milk
2 teaspoons instant cocoa mix

Marshmallows

1. Combine milk and cocoa in a 2-cup measuring cup.
2. Cook for 3½ minutes.
3. Add marshmallows and serve.

Slemp
4 servings

1 piece (1 inch) stick cinnamon
2 whole cloves
½ teaspoon ground mace
½ teaspoon instant tea

4 cups milk
Peel of half a lemon, cut in strips
⅛ teaspoon salt
2 tablespoons sugar

1. Tie cinnamon, cloves, mace, and tea in cheesecloth.
2. Place milk in a 2-quart casserole.
3. Add the bag of spices, lemon peel, and salt to milk.
4. Cook for 10 minutes.
5. Remove from oven and stir in sugar.
6. Cook for 1 minute.

Spicy Orange Coffee
6 servings

1 tablespoon sugar
6 whole cloves
2 pieces (1½ inches each) stick
cinnamon

Peel of small orange, in strips
1 tablespoon instant coffee

1. Combine all ingredients with 1½ cups water in a 2-cup measuring cup.
2. Heat for 8 minutes.
3. Strain into demitasse cups.

Café au Lait
4 servings

4 teaspoons instant coffee
2 cups milk

Sugar (optional)

1. Place coffee and 1 cup water in a 4-cup measuring cup.
2. Stir in milk.
3. Cook for 7 to 8 minutes.
4. Sweeten to taste, if desired.

Viennese After-Dinner Coffee
8 servings

6 teaspoons instant coffee

¼ cup heavy cream, whipped

1. Combine coffee and 3 cups water in a 4-cup measuring cup.
2. Cook for 7 to 8 minutes.
3. Serve in demitasse cups.
4. Top each serving with whipped cream.

Instant Coffee
4 servings

4 to 5 teaspoons instant coffee

1. Combine coffee and 3 cups water in a 1-quart measuring cup.
2. Cook for 7 to 8 minutes. To develop a richer flavor, let stand 2 minutes.

127

Coffee Cream Punch

8 servings

6 tablespoons instant coffee
1½ pints vanilla ice cream

Ground nutmeg

1. Combine coffee and 4 cups water in a 1½-quart casserole.
2. Cook for 6 to 7 minutes.
3. Meantime, place ice cream in a 3-quart bowl.
4. Pour hot coffee over the ice cream; stir until melted.
5. Ladle into cups and sprinkle each serving with nutmeg.

Café Calypso

6 servings

4 cups milk
⅓ cup instant coffee
¼ cup brown sugar

½ cup heavy cream, whipped
Ground nutmeg

1. Place ⅓ cup water in a 2-quart casserole.
2. Heat for 2 minutes.
3. Add milk, coffee, and sugar.
4. Cook for 10 minutes.
5. Serve hot, topped with whipped cream and a dash of nutmeg.

Hot Tea

4 servings

4 tea bags

1. Place 3 cups water in a 4-cup measuring cup.
2. Heat for 7 to 8 minutes.
3. Add tea bags. Remove when desired strength of tea is obtained.

Hot Instant Tea

4 servings

5 to 6 teaspoons instant tea

1. Mix tea with 3 cups water in a 4-cup measuring cup.
2. Heat for 7 to 8 minutes.

Iced Tea

4 servings

6 tea bags, or 2½ to 3 tablespoons
instant tea

3 to 4 tablespoons sugar
Ice cubes

1. Place 3 cups water in a 4-cup measuring cup.
2. Heat for 7 to 8 minutes.
3. Add tea.
4. When desired strength is obtained, take out tea bags and stir in sugar until dissolved.
5. Serve over ice in tall glasses.

Desserts

Your microwave oven will cook puddings, custards, fruits, and cakes superbly. Cake baking is much faster than conventionally, producing a cake with a different, but delectable, look and texture. Cakes should be rotated during cooking time so that they will rise evenly and produce a smooth top. Test with a toothpick; if it comes out clean, the cake is done. As it cools, the top, which looks somewhat damp, will dry out. You will be pleased with the moist texture and taste.

When baking double-crust fruit pies, cook in the microwave oven until the fruit is cooked—a great time-saver—then continue baking in the conventional oven until the crust is brown and crisp.

Applesauce Cake

12 servings

1 cup applesauce
⅞ cup brown sugar, firmly packed
½ cup melted butter or margarine
1¾ cups sifted all-purpose flour
1 teaspoon baking soda
½ teaspoon salt

1 teaspoon ground cinnamon
½ teaspoon ground cloves
1 teaspoon ground ginger
½ cup seedless raisins
½ cup chopped nuts

1. In a small bowl combine applesauce, sugar, and butter. Set aside.
2. Sift flour, baking soda, salt, and spices into a large mixing bowl. Add the applesauce mixture and blend well. Stir in raisins and nuts. Pour batter into a lightly greased 12- by 8- by 2-inch baking dish. Cover both ends of the baking dish with a strip of aluminum foil about 3 to 4 inches wide.
3. Cook for 7 minutes, rotating dish every 2 minutes.
4. Remove foil strips from ends of dish.
5. Cook for 8 minutes, or until done, rotating dish every 2 minutes. Cake is done when a toothpick inserted in center comes out clean.
6. Let cool before serving.

Devil's Food Cake

2 8-inch layers

2 cups sifted all-purpose flour
1¼ teaspoons baking soda
¼ teaspoon salt
½ cup shortening
2 cups sugar

½ cup cocoa
1 teaspoon vanilla extract
½ cup buttermilk
2 eggs, lightly beaten

1. Grease the bottoms of two 8-inch round cake dishes. Line the bottoms with 2 layers of waxed paper.
2. Sift together flour, baking soda, and salt. Set aside.
3. Cream together shortening, sugar, cocoa, and vanilla until light and fluffy.
4. Measure 1 cup water in a 2-cup measuring cup. Cook for 3½ to 4 minutes, or until water comes to a boil. Let stand.
5. Stir boiling water, buttermilk, and eggs into creamed mixture and beat well. Add sifted dry ingredients all at once and beat well.
6. Divide mixture between prepared cake dishes.
7. Ccok, uncovered, one layer at a time for 13 to 14 minutes, rotating every 3 minutes, to cook cake evenly.
8. Remove from oven and let stand until cake is cool.
9. Turn out of dishes and cool thoroughly. Frost as desired.

Gingerbread

6 to 8 servings

1 package (14 ounces) gingerbread mix

1. Prepare gingerbread mix according to package directions, decreasing liquid by 2 tablespoons. Pour batter into an 8-inch round cake dish.

2. Bake, uncovered, for 13 to 15 minutes, rotating dish every 2 minutes, or until a toothpick inserted in cake comes out clean.
3. Remove from oven and let stand a few minutes before cutting and serving.

Pumpkin Raisin-Nut Cake

12 servings

½ cup shortening
1 cup sugar
2 eggs, lightly beaten
1 cup solid-pack cooked pumpkin
2 cups sifted all-purpose flour
4 teaspoons baking powder
1 teaspoon baking soda

1 teaspoon salt
2½ teaspoons ground cinnamon
½ teaspoon ground nutmeg
¼ teaspoon ground ginger
1 cup seedless raisins
1 cup chopped nuts

1. Cream shortening and sugar together until light and fluffy. Beat in eggs and pumpkin; beat well.
2. Sift together flour, baking powder, baking soda, salt, and spices. Stir into pumpkin mixture and blend well. Stir in raisins and nuts. Pour batter into a lightly greased 12- by 8- by 2-inch baking dish. Cover both ends of the baking dish with a strip of aluminum foil about 3 to 4 inches wide.
3. Cook for 7 minutes, rotating dish every 2 minutes.
4. Remove foil strips from ends of dish.
5. Cook again for 8 minutes, or until done, rotating dish every 2 minutes. Cake is done when a toothpick inserted in center of cake comes out clean.
6. Let cool before serving.

Sour Cream Coffee Cake

1 8-inch cake

¼ cup butter or margarine
½ cup sugar
2 eggs
½ teaspoon vanilla extract
1½ cups sifted all-purpose flour
½ teaspoon baking soda
½ teaspoon baking powder

½ cup dairy sour cream
⅓ cup brown sugar, firmly packed
2 tablespoons flour
½ cup chopped nuts
⅛ teaspoon ground cinnamon
⅛ teaspoon salt
2 tablespoons butter or margarine

1. Cream together ¼ cup butter and sugar until light and fluffy. Add eggs and vanilla and beat thoroughly. Sift together flour, soda, and baking powder. Add to creamed mixture alternately with sour cream, blending well after each addition.
2. Combine remaining ingredients and mix until crumbly.
3. Spread half of the batter in an 8-inch round cake dish. Sprinkle with half of topping mix. Spread on remaining batter and sprinkle with remaining topping.
4. Cook for about 7½ to 8 minutes, rotating cake every 2 minutes so that it will bake evenly.

131

FOLLOWING PAGES: Left, *Gingerbread, page 130; Quick Boston Cream Pie and Pineapple Upside-Down Cake, page 135;* right, *Devil's Food Cake, page 130.*

Spice Cake

12 servings

2 eggs
1 cup sugar
2 tablespoons molasses
2 cups sifted all-purpose flour
1 teaspoon ground cinnamon
1 teaspoon ground cloves

½ teaspoon ground allspice
½ teaspoon salt
2 teaspoons baking powder
1 teaspoon baking soda
1 cup buttermilk
⅔ cup cooking oil

1. Beat eggs until thick and lemon-colored. Beat in sugar and molasses until well blended.
2. Sift together flour, spices, salt, baking powder, and baking soda. Add to egg mixture alternately with buttermilk, mixing well after each addition. Stir in oil.
3. Pour batter into a lightly greased 12- by 8- by 2-inch baking dish. Cover both ends of the baking dish with a strip of aluminum foil about 4 inches wide.
4. Cook for 7 minutes, rotating dish every 2 minutes.
5. Remove foil strips from ends of dish. Cook again for 8 minutes, or until done, rotating dish every 2 minutes. Cake is done when a toothpick inserted in center comes out clean.
6. Let cool before serving.

Packaged Cake Mix

3   8-inch layers

1 package (1 pound 2½ ounces) cake mix

1. Grease the bottom of an 8-inch round cake dish. Place two 8-inch circles of waxed paper on bottom of dish.
2. Prepare cake mix according to package directions, reducing liquid by about 2 tablespoons.
3. Pour one-third of the batter into the prepared cake dish.
4. Cook, uncovered, for 6 minutes, rotating dish every 2 minutes.
5. Let stand a few minutes to cool. Turn out of pan and remove waxed paper from bottom of cake.
6. Repeat process for 2 remaining layers.

Pound Cake

2 loaves

1 package (16 ounces) pound cake

1. Line the bottom of two 8- by 4-inch loaf pans with 2 layers of waxed paper.
2. Prepare cake mix according to package directions, reducing liquid by 2 tablespoons. Divide batter between 2 pans.
3. Cook, uncovered, 1 cake at a time, for 5 to 6 minutes, rotating loaf pan once during cooking period.
4. Let stand in cake pan 3 minutes. Turn out, peel off paper, and let cool before serving.

Pineapple Upside-Down Cake

6 servings

2 tablespoons butter or margarine

½ cup firmly packed dark brown sugar

1 can (8¼ ounces) sliced pineapple, well drained, juice reserved

6 to 10 maraschino cherries, well drained

1 package (9 ounces) yellow cake mix

Whipped cream

1. Put butter and brown sugar in an 8-inch square baking dish.
2. Cook, uncovered, for 2 to 2½ minutes, or until butter and sugar are blended.
3. Smooth mixture over bottom of pan. Arrange pineapple slices on brown sugar and dot with maraschino cherries.
4. Prepare package mix according to directions, using ⅓ cup of the pineapple juice for part of the liquid and reducing the total liquid by 1 tablespoon.
5. Pour batter carefully into pan without disturbing pineapple or sugar mixture.
6. Bake, uncovered, for 12 to 13 minutes, rotating pan every 3 minutes to brown evenly.
7. Remove from oven and let stand 3 minutes.
8. Invert pan on serving plate and remove pan, leaving syrup and fruit on top of cake.
9. Cut in squares and serve with whipped cream.

Quick Boston Cream Pie

1 8-inch pie

1 package Boston cream pie mix

1. Prepare pudding in package according to package directions. Set aside.
2. Grease the bottom of an 8-inch round cake dish. Place 2 circles of waxed paper on bottom of pan.
3. Prepare cake mix according to package directions, reducing liquid by 1 tablespoon.
4. Cook, uncovered, for 9 to 10 minutes, or until cake starts to come away from sides of pan and cake tester comes out clean.
5. Cool in pan about 3 minutes. Turn out of pan onto cake cooler and peel off waxed paper.
6. Assemble finished cake according to package directions.

Nut Bread Mix

1 loaf

1 package (17 ounces) nut bread mix

1. Line the bottom of a 9- by 5- by 3-inch loaf pan with 2 layers of waxed paper.
2. Prepare mix according to package directions, reducing liquid by about 2 tablespoons.
3. Pour into pan.
4. Bake, uncovered, for 14 to 16 minutes, rotating loaf about 4 times during cooking period.

135

FOLLOWING PAGES: Left, *Apple Pie;* right, *Cherry Cheese Pie;* page 139.

Corn Muffins

8 muffins

1 package (8½ ounces) corn bread or muffin mix

1. Place paper liners in 8 custard cups.
2. Prepare muffin mix according to package directions. Divide mixture among prepared cups, filling them not more than half full.
3. Bake, uncovered, for 2 to 2½ minutes, or until a toothpick inserted in center comes out clean.
4. Let stand a few minutes, then turn out of cups.

Another method:

1. Lightly grease the bottoms of 6 custard cups. Divide batter among prepared cups.
2. Bake for 3 minutes, alternating the position of the cups every 1 minute.

Cupcakes

8 cupcakes

1 package (8 ounces) yellow cake mix

1. Place paper liners in 8 custard cups.
2. Prepare cake mix according to package directions, reducing liquid by 1 tablespoon. Pour mixture into lined custard cups.
3. Place 4 cupcakes at a time in the oven, spaced about 1 inch apart. (Eight is too many and will not bake properly.)
4. Bake, uncovered, for 3 to 3½ minutes, rotating twice.
5. Remove from oven and let stand; allow tops to dry out slightly.
6. Frost as desired.

Another method:

1. Lightly grease the bottoms of 6 custard cups. Pour batter into cups.
2. Bake, uncovered, for 3½ to 4½ minutes.
3. Remove from oven. Let stand 2 minutes.
4. Turn cupcakes out and let cool upside down. Frost in this position.

Sticky Buns

6 servings

⅓ cup dark brown sugar, firmly packed **⅓ cup chopped nuts**
3 tablespoons butter or margarine **1 can (8 ounces) refrigerated biscuits**

1. Combine brown sugar, butter, and 1 tablespoon water in an 8-inch round baking dish.
2. Cook, uncovered, for 2 to 3 minutes, or until butter melts.
3. Stir mixture and spread over bottom of pan. Sprinkle nuts over top. Place biscuits on top of mixture.
4. Bake, uncovered, for 6 to 7 minutes, or until biscuits are firm and no longer doughy. Rotate pan 3 times during cooking period.
5. Let stand about 2 minutes. Invert on a flat serving plate.

Apple Pie

1 9-inch pie

7 medium apples
¾ cup sugar
2 tablespoons all-purpose flour
⅛ teaspoon salt
1 teaspoon ground cinnamon
¼ teaspoon ground nutmeg
1 recipe pie crust
1 to 2 teaspoons lemon juice
2 tablespoons butter

1. Pare and slice apples. Mix in a bowl with sugar, flour, salt, cinnamon, and nutmeg. Set aside.
2. Roll out half of the pie crust and fit in the bottom of a 9-inch pie dish. Put apples in pie crust. Sprinkle lemon juice over top if apples are not too tart. Dot with butter. Roll out remainder of pie crust and fit over apples. Seal edges and cut slits in top of pie.
3. Cook, uncovered, for 12 to 15 minutes, or until apples are tender.
4. While apples are cooking, preheat conventional oven to 450°.
5. When apples are tender, bake pie in conventional oven 12 to 14 minutes, or until crust is golden brown.
6. Serve warm or cold.

Note: The kind of pie crust that is used makes a difference in the browning time. Packaged pie crust mix browns faster than homemade.

Cherry Cheese Pie

1 9-inch pie

⅓ cup butter or margarine
1¼ cups graham cracker crumbs
¼ cup all-purpose flour
Sugar
1 package (8 ounces) cream cheese, softened
1 egg, lightly beaten
1 cup dairy sour cream, divided
1¾ teaspoons vanilla extract, divided
1 can (21 ounces) prepared cherry pie filling

1. Put butter in a 9-inch pie plate. Melt in oven, for 2 to 3 minutes.
2. Add graham cracker crumbs, flour, and 4 teaspoons sugar to melted butter in pie plate and blend well. Press mixture evenly over bottom and up sides of pie plate. Set aside.
3. Beat together softened cream cheese and ⅓ cup sugar until well blended. Add egg, ¼ cup sour cream, and ¾ teaspoon vanilla. Beat until light and fluffy. Pour into prepared graham cracker crust.
4. Cook, uncovered, for 4 minutes, turning once during cooking time.
5. Remove from oven and cool 8 minutes on a cooling rack.
6. Beat together ¾ cup sour cream with 2 tablespoons sugar and 1 teaspoon vanilla. Spoon carefully over top of cooked cheese mixture.
7. Cook, uncovered, for about 7 minutes, or just until sour cream is set.
8. Spoon cherry pie filling around edge of pie.
9. Chill thoroughly in refrigerator before serving.

139

FOLLOWING PAGES: Left, *Baked Custard*; right, *Old-Fashioned Indian Pudding*; page 143.

Custard Pie
(Special for Cholesterol Watchers)

1 9-inch pie

1 cup frozen cholesterol-free egg
   substitute, thawed
½ cup sugar
½ teaspoon salt

1 teaspoon vanilla extract
2 cups fat-free milk
1 9-inch baked pastry shell
Ground nutmeg

1. Beat together egg substitute, sugar, salt, vanilla, and milk. Remove ⅔ cup of the mixture and set aside. Pour remaining mixture into baked pastry shell.
2. Bake, uncovered, for 10 minutes.
3. Stir carefully to move the cooked portion from edge of pie to the center. Cook again, uncovered, for about 10 minutes, or until center of pie is almost set. Stir gently again if necessary, half way during cooking period.
4. Sprinkle top of pie with nutmeg and let cool before serving.

Note: Pour reserved custard mixture into 2 custard cups. Cook for 8 to 9 minutes, or just until mixture begins to boil. Cool before serving.

Pumpkin Pie

1 9-inch pie

2 eggs, lightly beaten
1½ cups solid-pack cooked pumpkin
¾ cup sugar
½ teaspoon salt
1 teaspoon ground cinnamon

½ teaspoon ground ginger
¼ teaspoon ground cloves
1 can (14½ ounces) evaporated milk
1 9-inch baked pastry shell

1. Combine eggs, pumpkin, sugar, salt, and spices and blend well. Stir in milk and make a smooth mixture.
2. Remove ⅔ cup of this mixture and set aside. Pour remaining mixture into baked pastry shell.
3. Cook for 10 minutes.
4. Stir very carefully to move the cooked portion from edge of pie to the center. Cook for 10 to 15 minutes, or until a knife inserted near the center comes out clean.
5. Let cool before cutting. Serve with flavored whipped cream, as top of pie may have a rough appearance.

Note: Pour reserved pumpkin mixture into custard cups, filling them three-quarters full. Cook for 8 to 9 minutes, or until a knife inserted near the center comes out clean.

Brandied Strawberry Sauce

1½ cups

1 pint fresh strawberries
1 cup sugar
1 tablespoon cornstarch

2 tablespoons lemon juice
2 tablespoons brandy

1. Clean and crush strawberries.

142

2. Combine sugar and cornstarch in a 1-quart mixing bowl. Stir in lemon juice and crushed strawberries.
3. Cook, uncovered, for about 7 minutes, or until mixture comes to a boil and is clear.
4. Cool slightly. Stir in brandy. Chill well before serving.

Baked Custard

5 to 6 servings

4 eggs
¼ cup sugar
¼ teaspoon salt

2 to 2½ cups milk
1 teaspoon vanilla extract
Ground nutmeg

1. Beat eggs until fluffy. Add sugar and salt and continue beating until thick and lemon-colored. Beat in milk and vanilla.
2. Pour mixture into five or six 6-ounce custard cups, filling about ¾ full. Sprinkle with nutmeg.
3. Arrange in oven with at least 1 inch of space between cups. Cook for 8 to 9 minutes, or just until custard begins to bubble. It may be necessary to remove a few of the custard cups and cook 1 or 2 cups about 30 seconds longer.
4. Remove and let stand to finish cooking.

Note: This custard can be baked in an 8-inch cake dish but the finished product will not be as even since the outside edge may become overcooked while the center is still soft and runny. However, if this method is desired, the cooking time is 25 to 26 minutes.

Old-Fashioned Indian Pudding

4 to 6 servings

2 cups milk, divided
¼ cup yellow cornmeal
2 tablespoons sugar
½ teaspoon salt
½ teaspoon ground cinnamon
¼ teaspoon ground ginger

1 egg, beaten
¼ cup molasses
1 tablespoon melted butter or
  margarine
Vanilla ice cream

1. Pour 1½ cups milk into a 1½-quart casserole. Heat for 5 minutes.
2. Combine cornmeal, sugar, salt, cinnamon, and ginger. Stir into hot milk.
3. Cook, uncovered, for 3 to 4 minutes, stirring at least once during cooking time.
4. Beat together egg, molasses, and butter. Stir a small amount of hot milk mixture into egg mixture. Return to casserole. Stir well.
5. Cook, uncovered, for 8 minutes, stirring every 2 minutes.
6. Pour remaining ½ cup cold milk carefully over top of pudding. *Do not stir.* Cook, uncovered, for 4 minutes, or until set.
7. Let stand 10 to 15 minutes before serving.
8. Serve warm topped with vanilla ice cream.

FOLLOWING PAGES: Left, *Baked Apples Supreme,* page 147; *Rhubarb Betty,* page 152.

Vanilla Mousse with Strawberry Sauce   8 to 10 servings

2 envelopes unflavored gelatin

1½ cups sugar, divided

1½ cups milk

2 eggs, separated

1 tablespoon vanilla extract

1 pint heavy cream, whipped

1 pint fresh strawberries

2 tablespoons cornstarch

½ cup lemon juice

2 tablespoons butter

1. Combine gelatin and 1 cup sugar in a mixing bowl and blend well. Stir in milk.
2. Cook, uncovered, for about 5 minutes, or until hot.
3. Beat egg yolks in a small dish. Gradually stir in a small amount of hot milk mixture. Add to large bowl of hot milk mixture. Blend well.
4. Cook, uncovered, for about 4 minutes, or just until bubbles form around edge of bowl. Do not overcook or mixture will curdle.
5. Stir in vanilla. Place bowl in a pan or bowl of ice water. Cool until custard mounds when dropped from a spoon.
6. Beat egg whites until stiff but not dry. Fold into custard mixture. Fold in whipped cream. Turn mixture into a 2-quart mold. Chill in the refrigerator until set.
7. To make the sauce: Clean and hull berries. Reserve 1 cup of the best berries for garnish. Force the remainder through a food mill, or blend in an electric blender. Put through a strainer to remove seeds.
8. Combine the remaining ½ cup sugar with cornstarch in a 1-quart mixing bowl. Gradually stir in 1 cup hot water.
9. Cook, uncovered, for about 7 minutes, or until mixture comes to a boil and is clear.
10. Stir in lemon juice, butter, and strawberry puree. Chill sauce.
11. Unmold mousse on a serving platter. Garnish with whole strawberries. Serve with chilled strawberry sauce.

Packaged Pudding Mix   4 servings

1 package (3¼ ounces) pudding mix, any flavor

2 cups milk

1. Combine pudding mix and milk in a 1-quart bowl or measuring cup. Blend well.
2. Cook, uncovered, for 10 to 12 minutes, stirring frequently during last 2 minutes of cooking time. Mixture will come to a boil and start to thicken during cooking period.
3. Remove from oven and stir well.
4. Pour into serving dishes and cool before serving.

Party-Pretty Pudding   8 servings

2 packages (3¼ ounces each) pudding mix, vanilla flavored

2 pints fresh strawberries, hulled, sliced, and sweetened

1. Prepare pudding according to preceding directions. Cool well.
2. In a pretty glass serving dish, spoon one-third of the cooled pudding. Cover with half the strawberries.
3. Repeat with a second layer of pudding and the remaining strawberries. Spoon the remaining third of the pudding on top of the strawberries. Top with sweetened whipped cream if desired.
4. Chill well before serving.

Note: If desired, the layers may be made in individual serving dishes.

Quick Crème Brûlée   4 servings

1 package (3¼ ounces) pudding mix,   **Brown sugar**
vanilla flavor

1. Prepare pudding mix according to preceding directions. Pour cooked pudding into a flat baking dish. Cool well and chill.
2. Sift a layer of brown sugar, about ⅛ inch thick, over top of pudding, making sure to cover entire top.
3. Place under a hot broiler and broil until sugar melts and bubbles. Watch carefully so that sugar does not burn.

Baked Apples Supreme   6 servings

6 baking apples   **¼ cup brown sugar**
Lemon juice   **2 teaspoons ground cinnamon**
½ cup slivered almonds   **6 teaspoons butter or margarine**
¼ cup raisins

1. Wash apples and remove core, making a generous cavity in each apple. Remove thin circle of peel around cavity and sprinkle with lemon juice.
2. Mix together almonds, raisins, brown sugar, and cinnamon. Fill cavities with mixture and place each apple in a small custard dish. Put 2 tablespoons of water in dish around apple. Dot each apple with 1 teaspoon butter.
3. Cook for 8 minutes.
4. Let stand 2 to 3 minutes before serving.

Quick Peach Delight   4 servings

4 large canned peach halves   **4 teaspoons brown sugar**
1¼ teaspoons butter or margarine **Vanilla ice cream**

1. Drain peaches thoroughly. Place in a 1-quart baking dish. Put ¼ teaspoon butter in center of each peach. Sprinkle 1 teaspoon brown sugar on each peach half.
2. Bake, uncovered, for 5 minutes, or until piping hot.
3. Serve warm with a small scoop of ice cream in center of each peach half.

147

FOLLOWING PAGES: Left, *Party-Pretty Pudding, page 146;* right, *Butterscotch Sauce and Fancy Chocolate Sauce, page 152, used on a banana split.*

Quick Applescotch

1 can (1 pound) pie-sliced apples
½ package (6 ounces) butterscotch flavored morsels
1 tablespoon quick-cooking tapioca
½ tablespoon lemon juice
¼ cup all-purpose flour
¼ cup sugar
½ teaspoon ground cinnamon
¼ cup firm butter or margarine

1. Combine apples, butterscotch morsels, and tapioca in a 1-quart casserole. Sprinkle lemon juice over the top.
2. Combine flour, sugar, and cinnamon in a small bowl. Cut in butter with a pastry blender or two knives until mixture resembles cornmeal. Sprinkle over top of apple mixture.
3. Cook, uncovered, for 10 to 12 minutes, or until piping hot.
4. Serve warm with heavy cream or ice cream, if desired.

Cranberry Apple Crunch

6 servings

1 cup sugar
2 cups chopped cranberries
2 cups chopped apples
1 cup quick-cooking rolled oats
½ cup firmly packed brown sugar
⅓ cup all-purpose flour
½ teaspoon salt
¼ cup butter or margarine
½ cup chopped nuts

1. Combine sugar, 1 cup water, cranberries, and apples in a buttered 2-quart casserole or baking dish.
2. Cook, covered, for 10 to 12 minutes, or until apples are tender.
3. Mix together oats, sugar, flour, and salt. Cut in butter with two knives to make a coarse mixture. Stir in nuts. Sprinkle over top of cranberry mixture.
4. Cook, covered, for 10 to 12 minutes, or until topping and apples are done.
5. Let stand 3 to 4 minutes before serving. Serve with whipped cream.

Apple Betty

6 servings

⅓ cup melted butter or margarine
2 cups fresh bread crumbs
6 cups sliced, peeled, and cored cooking apples
½ cup firmly packed brown sugar
½ teaspoon ground nutmeg
¼ teaspoon ground cinnamon
1 tablespoon grated lemon peel (optional)
2 tablespoons lemon juice

1. Toss melted butter with bread crumbs. Put one-third of the buttered bread crumbs in a 2-quart casserole.
2. Combine apples with brown sugar, nutmeg, cinnamon, and lemon peel. Put half of the apple mixture on bread crumbs layer. Cover with one-third of the crumbs. Add remaining apples.
3. Combine lemon juice and ¼ cup water. Pour over apples. Top with remaining buttered crumbs.
4. Cook, covered, for 15 to 17 minutes.
5. Remove cover and cook again for 15 minutes, or until apples are tender.

Stewed Apricots

½ pound dried apricots
1 cup white raisins
Juice of 1 lemon, or 2 tablespoons
  lemon juice

½ cup sugar
1 can (11 ounces) mandarin oranges,
  drained

1. Rinse apricots and raisins in water. Drain.
2. Put apricots and raisins in a 1½-quart casserole. Add 1½ cups water and cook, uncovered, for 8 minutes.
3. Add lemon juice, sugar, and mandarin oranges. Return to oven and cook for 8 minutes. Let stand 2 or 3 minutes before serving, or chill.

Baked Maple Bananas

2 tablespoons butter or margarine
3 tablespoons maple syrup

4 bananas
Lemon juice

1. Place butter in a medium-size baking dish. Cook for 1½ minutes, or until butter is melted.
2. Add maple syrup and mix.
3. Place peeled bananas in dish and spoon butter mixture over so that bananas are well coated. Cook for 3½ minutes. Turn bananas completely over once, halfway through cooking.
4. Remove from oven and sprinkle with lemon juice.

Honeyed Blueberries

3 cups bran flakes
½ cup honey
¼ cup sugar

1 teaspoon ground cinnamon
½ teaspoon ground nutmeg
2 cups fresh blueberries

1. In a bowl, combine bran flakes, honey, sugar, cinnamon, and nutmeg.
2. Grease an 8-inch square baking dish. Spread half the bran flakes mixture on the bottom. Cover with half the blueberries. Cover blueberries with remaining bran flakes and top with remaining blueberries.
3. Cook, covered, for 7 minutes. Serve hot, topped with ice cream.

Date-Filled Pears

4 fresh Bartlett pears
½ cup pitted dates, cut in small pieces
2 tablespoons light brown sugar

3 tablespoons butter or margarine
⅓ cup dry vermouth

1. Cut pears in half. Peel and core. Place in baking dish, cut-side up.
2. Fill pear centers with cut dates. Sprinkle with brown sugar and dot with butter.
3. Pour vermouth over pears and cook, uncovered, for 12 minutes. Baste with vermouth at least twice during cooking. Let stand 2 or 3 minutes.

Fresh Rhubarb Betty

6 to 8 servings

6 cups diced fresh rhubarb
1¼ cups sugar
2½ tablespoons quick-cooking tapioca
1 teaspoon grated lemon peel

1 tablespoon grated orange peel
2¾ cups soft bread cubes
⅓ cup butter or margarine
1 teaspoon vanilla extract

1. Combine rhubarb, sugar, tapioca, lemon peel, and orange peel in a bowl. Set aside.
2. Put bread cubes in a bowl.
3. Place butter in a measuring cup. Cook, covered, for 1 minute, or until butter melts.
4. Pour butter over bread cubes; add vanilla and toss lightly.
5. In a 1½-quart casserole make alternate layers of rhubarb and bread-cube mixture, ending with buttered bread cubes.
6. Cook, covered, for 15 to 17 minutes, or until rhubarb is cooked.
7. Serve warm or chilled.

Butterscotch Sauce

1 cup

½ cup sugar
½ cup firmly packed dark brown sugar
½ cup light cream

1 teaspoon vanilla extract
2 tablespoons butter
⅛ teaspoon salt

1. Combine all ingredients in a 2-cup measuring cup.
2. Cook, uncovered, for 5 minutes, or until sauce is well blended and hot, stirring once.
3. Serve warm over ice cream.

Fancy Chocolate Sauce

2 cups

1 package (12 ounces) semisweet chocolate bits
2 squares (2 ounces) unsweetened chocolate

1 cup heavy cream
3 tablespoons brandy

1. Combine chocolate bits and unsweetened chocolate in a small mixing bowl.
2. Cook, covered, for 5 minutes, or just until chocolate melts. Watch carefully during last 1 minute so that it does not burn.
3. Stir in cream with a wire whisk to make a smooth paste.
4. Cook, covered, for about 1 to 1½ minutes, or until hot.
5. Stir in brandy.
6. Serve hot over vanilla ice cream or cake squares.

OPPOSITE: *The microwave oven heats frozen foods perfectly, page 154.*

Heating times for frozen cooked foods

Meat Loaf (2 pounds)

1. Heat for 5 minutes. Let stand 2 to 3 minutes.
2. Heat for 5 minutes. Let stand 2 to 3 minutes.
3. Heat for 5 minutes. Let stand 2 to 3 minutes.
4. Heat for 6 minutes, or until piping hot.

Cooked Chicken (cut in pieces)

1. Place each piece of chicken on a dinner plate.
2. Heat 2 to 3 pieces at a time for 7 to 8 minutes.
3. If only 1 piece of chicken is desired, heat for 4 minutes.

Spaghetti Sauce (1 pint)

1. Place plastic container in microwave oven 1 to 2 minutes to loosen sauce. Place sauce in a 1-quart casserole.
2. Cook for 16 to 20 minutes, stirring 3 or 4 times during heating period.

Cooked Rice (10-ounce package)

1. Make a slit in top of bag, and place bag in oven.
2. Heat for 10 minutes, rearranging rice in bag by poking or squeezing bag once during cooking period.

Chili con Carne (1 quart)

1. Place plastic container in microwave oven 1 to 2 minutes to loosen chili. Turn chili into a 1½-quart casserole.
2. Heat, covered, for 25 to 30 minutes, or until hot, stirring 3 to 4 times.
3. Let stand 3 minutes before serving.

Potatoes au Gratin (10-ounce package)

1. Turn out of aluminum pan into small casserole or serving dish.
2. Heat, covered, for 12 minutes, stirring once or twice during cooking period.

Macaroni and Cheese (10-ounce package)

1. Turn out of aluminum pan into small casserole or serving dish.
2. Heat, covered, for 10 minutes, stirring once or twice.

TV Dinner (2-course type, frozen flat)

1. Leave dinner in tray. Remove foil from top and cover dinner with waxed paper.
2. Heat for 12 to 13 minutes.

Note: Chinese TV dinners are not recommended for heating by this method, as the shrimp they usually contain will burn. Meat dinners are the best kind to use in the microwave oven.

INDEX